why old men weep in the morning

Gary A. Westgard

they are already beginning to miss this world

Then the Lord said, "My spirit shall not abide in mortals forever, for they are flesh; their days shall be one hundred twenty years." Genesis 6:3

Copyright © 2024

Written by Gary A. Westgard
Edited by John Andrews
Designed by Andrea Maibaum

All rights reserved. No part of this publication may be reproduced without written permission by the author's family, except for purposes of review by academia, publications or broadcast.

Published by
South Dakota Magazine

DEDICATION

To Vivian always

AN APPRECIATION

*Thanks to Bernie Hunhoff, John Andrews,
Andrea Maibaum and all the* South Dakota Magazine
staff for their kindness and guidance.

Do not cast me off in the time of old age;
do not forsake me when my strength is spent.
Psalm 71:9

Foreword

As I jot these lines down for you, I work under the assumption that you never met Gary Westgard. And in that case, you also never witnessed the deep love for his wife Vivian and his family, his profound faith, his marvelous wit, and his gracious presence.

I, on the other hand, had the honor to personally know Gary, first as a first call pastor, then as a cherished colleague and later as his bishop. Most importantly, Gary always received and met me as his friend.

Words to Gary were like seasoned friends. He sought them out thoughtfully and tended to them intently. Over a lifetime, familiarity between them grew; they explored deep truths together, gained surprising insights, discovered humorous sides to life and captured tender vulnerabilities of our world.

The legacy of their lifelong adventure is what you now hold in your hands. Through this book you will get to know Gary, but most notably, you will discover anew who you are in this world as God's beloved creation. I will to you Gary Westgard.

— Bishop Constanze Hagmaier
South Dakota Synod
Evangelical Lutheran Church in America

Again, Again

She takes the child to the park just down the block. The child is excited because she has been there before, and she remembers. Mom picks her up so she can get her bottom on the board, then grabs the ropes and pulls the swing back. Not too far. Too far and her daughter will become afraid. She lets go and the swing does its job. She shrieks just a bit and then the laughter follows. As she comes back, mom gives her a slight push. They do this together for ten minutes, then mom grabs the ropes and gently brings the swing to a stop.

It is then that the little girl pleads, "Again, again. Let's do it again."

The old man looks back upon his life. Blessed beyond measure. Parents who loved him, forgave him, encouraged him. Sisters who became friends. A most beautiful wife who loved him just the way he was. Two children who grew up to be good human beings. Two grandsons who make him proud. Work that gave him joy. Friends who laughed with him.

But it is almost time to be done and so he prays, "Again, again. Let's do it again."

The Choices We Make on This Journey Called Life

I used to say that I had more time than money. I am not sure that is true anymore.

To live long upon this earth as a person of faith is to understand that faith is not magic, that life can be hard, even for those who believe in and follow Jesus, that loss comes to everyone, that our time on this earth passes too quickly, and that death, this last enemy, is not always so scary.

My father lived to the age of 85. He had outlived his wife, most of his siblings and friends and had given up driving. Life was no longer that interesting for him. I lived in the Midwest, and he lived on the West Coast. We mostly visited by phone. One day he said, "All I want to do is go to sleep and not wake up again." Shortly after, that is basically what happened.

We see life and think differently when we have more years behind than ahead. When I visited people in care centers and nursing homes, I found that they rarely spoke about jobs held or money made. Not a one said, "Oh how I wish I would have worked harder." Rather, they spoke about their parents, siblings, spouse, children, grandchildren. They told of the people they missed because they were and still are important to them. More important than a job or income or prestige.

I once read about a priest who wrote about his dying, about the cancer that had come into his body, and he said that if he had been given the opportunity to choose how to die, this is what he would choose, for the cancer gave him time to say goodbye to the people he loved.

What that priest and these older saints I visited are saying is that life is about relationships, about being loved and loving the other people we meet on this journey called life.

Vivian and I built a house after I retired. We liked it, but if we could do it again, we would do some things differently. I think a person has to build a house about three times before getting it right.

In this life that we are given, we get one chance to get it right. One chance. No doubt most of us, perhaps all of us, would say, "If I had to do it over again, I would …."

I believe my older friends would finish that sentence with words about family, thanking their parents, keeping in touch with brothers and sisters, telling their spouse more often of their love, about … well, you get it.

Having Reached a Certain Age

I have come to the realization,
having reached a certain age,
there are some things I will
never do.
So there will come a day
when people may
stand at my grave and say,
He never did learn
how to swim, did he?
There was a time when
I could think,
maybe I will do that.
Someday.
But I have come to an age
when I realize
there are some things
I will never do.
I will never again walk to the rim
of that mountain called St. Helens,
nor see my poems
in the New Yorker magazine.
But I have also
come to the realization,
having reached a certain age,
other things are also true.
I will never have to wonder
if I am loved,
nor worry that in the end
I will be alone.

I Used to Wonder

I used to wonder how is it
to be old?
Now I know.
In truth,
it really is no different
than being young,
in many ways,
in the important ways.
Except, of course,
in the eyes of the young.
I remember thinking the way
they think.
The young say,
Now that you are retired,
you have all this time
to do whatever you please.
But time is exactly what
the old do not have.
The young throw time away.
For the old, time is precious,
something to be hoarded.
I get greedy about time.
And old friends.
They keep leaving, you see.

If I Could Go Back

I suppose it happens to all of us.
We simply are incapable of knowing.
Until we trade places.
Until we are no longer the child.
Until we become the parent of the child.
Perhaps then we see the truth of how we were.
When I consider my own children,
I wonder why they do not ask:
How was it when you were a child?
How did you meet?
Did you ever doubt yourself?
Were you ever afraid?
If I could go back,
I would ask to hear the stories
and about falling in love.
If I could go back,
I would ask, *What was it like*
when you were me?
And I would listen more.
If I could go back,
I would listen to their lives
before I was me.

I Have Gotten Old

So there are things I do not do anymore.
I have said no to weddings,
traveling to other communities to lead worship.
But I do believe there is one thing
I can continue to do, or at least strive to do.
I can still bless people.
So that is my job now ...
to bless people.
I use words.

Her Wish

Her days are spent in a wheelchair,
living in a place she would rather not be.
Her husband died last February.
Married for over 60 years.
I wish I could have died when
he died, she says,
and means it.
I picked him out, she says.
We were skating.
It was ladies' choice,
and I picked him out.
We have been together
ever since.
I wish I could have died
when he died.

She Forgets

It troubles her.
There is this desire
to fix it, make it better,
but no one knows how.
So it is her present and
her future.
It is and it will be
this way now.
To forget one's keys
or an appointment,
is frustrating.
But this is something else.
This losing of self,
of one's recent past.
The childhood is there,
but yesterday is gone.
Birthdays and family
are in the mind,
but this morning's
conversation has
disappeared.
Pieces of life
gone. But where?
She remembers
that she forgets,
and therein lies
the sorrow.

We Still Have Our Voices

I believe Psalm 71 was written by an older man or woman who prays, "My mouth is filled with your praise, and with your glory all day long. Do not cast me off in the time of old age; do not forsake me when my strength is spent. O God, from my youth you have taught me, and I still proclaim your wondrous deeds. So even to old age and gray hairs, O God, do not forsake me, until I proclaim your might to all the generations to come."

We still have our voices.

I recently received a phone call from an old college buddy. I am pretty sure his body is not in much better shape than mine. But his voice is the same. He still has that same voice from over 50 years ago.

So we may not hear so well, but we still have our voices. We may not be able to run or hurry up the stairs, but we still have our voices.

Voices of comfort and hope and encouragement. We can still protest. We can still compliment. We can still tell another of our love. We can still teach. We can still pray.

Because we still have our voices.

Listening to Elvis or Usher, Glenn Miller or Taylor Swift

Vivian and I were preparing lunch. She took a pear, cut it in half, then moaned. "Look, it's black inside. I should have eaten it sooner when it was fresh. I like my food fresh. I don't like old food. I don't like anything old."

I thought, well that certainly does not bode well for me.

Recently we traveled to Luther Seminary in St. Paul, Minnesota. We gathered with other members of the class of 1969 to celebrate our golden anniversary. There were about 100 in our class, and when we gathered, we held a memorial service for 38 classmates.

For the past several years our class has held reunions. We have gotten to know one another as old people, so we learn of the cancer, hearing aids, Parkinson's, hip surgery, memory loss.

Besides the fact that we are all pretty old and frequently reminded of our mortality, we also deal with retirement in different ways. Some got used to the idea in a couple of minutes. Others have a more difficult time.

I don't know this for sure, but my best guess is that for some there is the real sense that they no longer have anything to contribute, they no longer have value. Maybe some of you reading these words understand that.

Psalm 71 is the prayer of an older person, asking that God not forget. "Do not cast me off in the time of old age; do not forsake me when my strength is spent." Then these words: "So even to old age and gray hairs, O God, do not forsake me."

What I say now has been said by others with greater knowledge and insight, but hear it again. If you can identify with me and my seminary classmates, if you are of the same vintage, know that you do have value, that you do have much to contribute. We have what the young do not yet have. We have lived. We have experience. Oh, we may have trouble with technology, but we know something about humanity, about sadness and joy, loss and death. We have some understanding about what counts finally, what is important in life and what can be tossed aside.

We have gained wisdom. That might not count for much when it comes to working the remote control but is a wonderful contribution when it comes to relationships. Is there perfection in us? Certainly not. We, too, are mighty sinners. But I noticed something at our St. Paul reunion. We laughed. We laughed a lot. We laughed at ourselves and with one another. I heard no unkind word spoken, no complaint about another's presentation or question. We were kind to each other. We no longer had to prove anything or ask for approval. Not a bad lesson to learn early in life.

When we first enter this world, there is no expectation that we do anything to receive attention and affection. We are loved and cared for by just being. We are receivers, and nothing more. I suggest that some of us will leave this world in the same way. Our bodies and our minds worn out, so we have nothing left to give. But we still are, and by just being, we still have value. You came into this world a child of God, created in the very image of God. That image does not fade with the passing of years. There may be lines on your face reflecting years of hard work and hard learning, but you are still God's little one, precious and loved.

If you, dear reader, are not yet at this place in life, then may these words encourage you to take note of those in your family or neighborhood who are, who would rather listen to Glenn Miller or Elvis (who would be celebrating his 85th birthday next January) than Taylor Swift (a mere 30 in December) or Usher. Take note of these older folks and allow them to bring to the table of life what they have to offer: experience, wisdom, laughter and some spare time.

You may not want to ask us old people to fix your computer or program your smartphone, but we could help with some insights into how to raise kids, get along with your brother-in-law, live on a tight budget or not take yourself too seriously.

We will tell you that life really is short, so pay attention to what counts. Pay attention to things like love, joy, peace, patience, kindness, generosity, faithfulness, gentleness and self-control.

You don't need an app for any of the above. They are bestowed upon us from above, from the God who created all things to be good. They are gifts, not to be stored for later, but best opened and used daily.

A few years ago, while visiting our son in Silver Spring, Maryland, we took the Metro to the Washington Mall. On the way home I got separated from Vivian and our daughter, so I rode the train alone. I asked a woman sitting nearby about the station where I would exit the train. She told me which stop my station would follow. Then a man sitting next to her said, "I will tell you when we get to the station you need." He did. I knew I would never see this good gentleman again, so as I got up to leave I touched his shoulder and said, "Have a good life."

It is what I say to you today, wherever you are on this journey. Have a good life.

Pastor Standing Next to the Mother of the Bride

— for Linda Iverson

The candles have been lit.
The widowed grandmother
has been walked down the
aisle by her grandson, the groom,
who then guides the other grandparents
to their places up front.
The groom has two more trips,
one with his parents,
then the final walk with the mother of the bride.
I stand next to this woman who
has watched her oldest son
get married and move two states away,
and who will soon sit helplessly as her
only daughter joins herself to this man
who is now coming back up the aisle,
to take her to a place she is not sure
she wants to go.
She turns to me and says,
I'm not going.
I understand.
I stood, in the afternoon, in the empty
bedroom of a daughter delivered to
college that same morning, remembering
another morning when she walked off to
kindergarten with the neighbor girl.
I turned my back on the airplane taking
our son over the ocean, and sat wiping
tears next to his mother in the front row

as he spoke promises to his young bride.
Every new place we enter,
every new walk we take, brings
with it a guarantee: it will not be
as it once was, not ever again.
So on this warm October afternoon,
when the mother of the bride
says, I'm not going, I turn to
her and say, *Good, if you're not
going, I'm not going either*. And then
we both go.

Do not let loyalty and faithfulness forsake you;
bind them around your neck ...
Proverbs 3:3

Home Again

I wait each day,
while away from home,
for evening to come,
when all our work is done.
Then I walk with purpose
to the one phone
in the building,
hoping no one has walked
faster than I.
I punch eleven numbers.
She answers,
700 miles away.
For the next 10 minutes
I am home again.
For she is my home.

Married Long

It is not the same passion,
but it is passion nonetheless.
It is the passion of being with,
of shared secrets,
long periods of
comfortable silence.
The passion of
knowing the
faults of the other
and still being friends.
The passion of
being safe
with this one
always, always.
No fear, except
that it will end. One will
leave and the other
will be alone.
One flesh
torn apart.

It Takes Two of Us

Mostly it is about forgetting.
Either I am forgetting something
or she is forgetting something.
So we have come to this conclusion:
It takes two of us to be one
almost fully functioning
human being.

Death Steals the Precious

The chair greets the guest,
Revealing the vacancy of a room
And related lives.
Still and secret as the night,
Death steals the precious
And fills the house with emptiness.
Large and capable hands now rest,
A voice no longer heard,
Familiar, smiling, laughing voice
Forever gone. A life spent.
Spent lavishly, willingly, wisely.
Wealthy with children and friends.
No hoarding, hiding, hollow.
The account is full,
Not now empty from life.
Memory and gratitude purchased
In the spending.
He like an oak tree,
She like a rose.
The rose shading the oak.
The oak fallen,
The rose remains, lonely, lonely,
Facing the empty chair,
Calling, calling the name.

The Auction

We crowd around the hay wagon,
like hungry puppies, while two
men stand looking down upon us,
one pointing a finger at an old friend,
the other doing a sound check on the
portable microphone, both trying
their best not to step on the boxes,
full of dishes, old tools, mason jars,
which will be sold first, then moving
on to the larger items, four matching
chairs, a sewing machine that hasn't
been used for a generation, an iron
bed, a 100-year-old stone crock jar, no
cracks or chips, a kitchen cupboard
with the original light stain turned
dark by the passing of time, and
finally the John Deere tractor, pulled
in from the trees at the back of the
house, which will soon be hauled
away to be set in someone's barn or
garage, shined and tuned, ready for
the next small-town parade, driven
by the new owner's grandson, and
we do not notice that the owners of
the boxes and chairs and the green
tractor are not among us, but inside
the house, afraid of revealing the
sadness they know this day, for the
neighbors gathered here only know
that the old couple will move into
an apartment in town, with no road

to clear in the winter, no yard to tend,
no chores to finish before bedtime,
and they are glad for them and do not,
cannot, understand the great grief they
feel this day as their lives are held up
before neighbors and strangers and sold
to the highest bidder, that what is being
sold today is not merely tools and furniture
and dishes, but fifty years of living, piled
unto a hay wagon, carried out to the front
yard, and while anxious buyers count
plates and cups, lift up a flower vase
to find a name, pull out a drawer to see
how it was cut, nobody says a prayer
for the two people inside the old house,
now walking through each room, their
footsteps echoing in the empty space,
now stopping to embrace.

My maternal grandfather, Gunder Olson, was born in 1891. He died in 1992 at the age of 101. Selma was also born in 1891. She died in 1980 at the age of 89. They were both 24 when they married and they were married for 65 years — a long time, it would seem, but it is never long enough.

She's an Old Tree

>Gunder (Gunnar) Olson &
>Selma Marie Haldorsen, 1915-1980

She's an old tree, branches bare,
some broken. The ground below
receiving the life that used to be.
One day she got tired and tried to
lie down, came to rest against
the tree nearest. Since the
beginning, they have stood
next to one another, deeply rooted.
I stop now on this road to listen.
I hear him. *It's alright, I
can hold you like this forever,
I won't let you fall.*

It is my grandfather whispering to my
grandmother when she could no longer
care for herself, and he kept her in their
home until she died, never left her alone,
									never let her fall.

Children are a heritage from the L<small>ORD</small>,
offspring a reward from him.
Psalm 127:3

Not Yet

He looks to be about four years old.
He is following his father from the
playground to his house just across.
He is angry, no doubt about it.
His cry can be heard in the closing of the day.
When he is older, he will run back to the play.
But now he follows his father.
Angry? Yes.
But still he stays close.
Not yet will he run from.
Not yet will he go off alone.
Not yet will he defy his father.
Not yet.
Now he follows. Still angry. Still crying.
But he follows.
It will not always be so.

Where the Children Play

We are walking the track
above the gym
where the children play.
We hear their sound.
Excited conversations.
High pitched giggles
of joy. They run
and run
and run.
They run
as children run,
with seemingly
no effort.
The adults come.
They place balls
on the floor,
perhaps 20 or more.
A whistle is
blown.
At the sound,
some children
run to the balls.
Some children
run away.
Some children
wait and watch.
Some children
take a ball
in each hand.
Some children
take only one.

It begins.
Children throwing
balls at children.
Loud music plays.
The adults
lean against the wall,
arms folded.
Like politicians
far away safe.

*Then the little children were being brought to him
in order that he might lay his hands on them and pray.
The disciples spoke sternly to those who brought
them; but Jesus said, "Let the little children come
to me, and do not stop them; for it is to such as
these that the kingdom of heaven belongs."*

Matthew 19:13-15

Right Outside My Door

I am sitting in my favorite chair
reading the afternoon paper
when I hear the sound of the
kingdom of heaven.
I go to the window
and there,
right there,
on the sidewalk
in front of my house,
the kingdom of heaven,
riding their bikes,
running,
giggling,
telling secrets,
having a great time,
right outside my door.

The Laughter

This morning
we heard from
both of our children.
So it is already
a good day.
It seems now
so long ago,
when they were
going off to school
for the first time,
struggling with homework,
fighting in the back seat,
learning to drive,
sleeping upstairs.
At the time,
it seemed it would
go on forever:
the homework,
the driving lessons,
friends coming over,
the noise.
It is quiet now,
except when they
come home.
I would not wish
them back,
nor would they.
But I am glad
for the memories
and the laughter
of that time
long ago.

Teaching Our Children How to Drive

I was sitting in the front seat, passenger side, next to one of our children who was driving. Vivian was on the floor in the back seat, fearing for her life.

After Christin got her driver's license, she and some friends went to Sioux City. It was our daughter's first trip out of town. As we waved goodbye, we both admitted we were worried.

But what do we do about it? There is really nothing. We taught her as best we could. She is a responsible person. Now we let her go.

And we worried.

Lewis Thomas (1913-1993) wrote: "We are, perhaps, uniquely among the earth's creatures, the worrying animal. We worry about our lives, fearing the future, discontent with the present, unable to take in the idea of dying, unable to sit still."

And Jesus says, "Therefore I tell you, do not worry about your life, what you will eat or what you will drink, or about your body, what you will wear. Do not worry about tomorrow, for tomorrow will bring worries of its own. Today's trouble is enough for today." He also asks, "Can any of you by worrying add a single hour to your span of life?" Matthew 6

These words convey God's concern for us. They are not so much a command as they are a truth. Worrying will not change anything. Jesus wants what any parent wants for their child. Jesus is saying, I want you to enjoy life, to know of my care for you, and to know that worry does not really change anything, will not guarantee the results you desire.

But we still worry.

Jumping

I watch my grandsons
as they jump on the couch,
jump down unto the floor,
jump back up again.
With seemingly no effort.
Jump up and jump down.
It seems unfair, to tell the truth.
Should we not have to learn jumping?
Should it not come later in life?
After living for a while upon this earth?
Should it not come after years
of practice and several
rehearsals?
Perhaps an apprenticeship
with an older jumper?
Or after some college classes?
Maybe an undergraduate
degree in jumping?
Why should it come
so easy for them?
Why should it be that they,
so young, just beginning life,
without any practice,
with no teaching whatsoever,
should be able
to do something
their grandfather,
cannot do?
I would speak with them
about it, but
they have just
jumped away.

The Look

It is Sunday morning.
Mother's Day.
Worship.
Just before we begin,
Grandmother leads
her daughter
and two grandsons
into the pew just
ahead.
The boys appear to
be in their teens.
They have known
one another their whole lives.
They are comfortable close.
They sit polite and still.
No sound coming from either.
But then it begins.
A poke here. A jab there.
A quiet kind of
wrestling match.
Who would notice?
Grandma.
Not a word is spoken.
Not a hand is raised.
Just the look.
It speaks volumes.
And it does its work.
Praise God for
grandmothers,
unafraid.

But Jesus Says

They say I am too small to play
That I'm not pretty or bright
They say I am different because I am gay
They say my thinking's not right
They say, they say, they say
But Jesus says, I am a child of God

They say my skin is too black
That my religion's all wrong
They say why don't you go back
go back to where you belong
They say, they say, they say
But Jesus says, I am a child of God

They say I don't talk like they do
They say be like the rest of us
See the world from our point of view
don't fight it, don't make such a fuss
They say, they say, they say
But Jesus says, I am a child of God

Yes, I am a child of God
Created in the very image
I am a child of God
A masterpiece God did finish
No matter what anyone else may say
Jesus says, I am a child of God

Family Valuables

In Matthew chapter 6, Jesus says, "For where your treasure is, there will your heart be also." Another translation puts it this way: "The place where your treasure is, is the place you will most want to be, or end up being."

A woman hired a nanny to care for her child. The child noticed that each time the parents got ready to leave their daughter with the nanny, they locked away some of their small antiques and jewelry. The daughter asked her mother, why? The mother said that she did not know yet if she could trust the new nanny with the family valuables.

The daughter then asked the obvious question: "Am I a family valuable?"

Territory

Bernie was our neighbor. She was four years old. We lived near a park with swings and a slide. One day as we drove by the park, I thought I saw Bernie climbing up the slide. I pointed her out to Vivian, who said, "I wonder if it's her because I don't see her mom."

A few days later I visited with mom. She said that she had been reading the *Fancy Nancy* books to Bernie, and one of them is about the word "territory." So mom asked Bernie, "What is your territory?" Bernie said, "Our home and Meesters (another neighbor) and Vivian and Gary." Mom told me that Bernie had left her territory, then got hurt on the slide and came home crying.

Jesus is saying the same thing. Stay close to me. Trust me. Listen to me. Learn from me. Know that I am already close to you. I am already listening to you. I am already trusting you. I have entrusted my church to you. I have entrusted the poor to you. I have entrusted my children to you. Abide in me as I abide in you.

Jesus is our territory.

Walking My Grandsons to School

Up ahead a woman
wearing a housecoat is
saying goodbye to a child.
Perhaps a grandchild
who spent the night
with Grandma.
She turns as we come
up behind her,
then smiles
this beautiful smile.
We greet
one another,
then go on our way.
I have never
seen her before.
I will not see her again.
But in this one moment
we share
this world,
this life.
Two children of God
wishing one another
a good day.
And it is.

Some friends play at friendship
but a true friend sticks closer than one's nearest kin.
Proverbs 18:24

A Few Words in Praise of Friendship

Every Tuesday morning at 10. It's on the calendar. Other things must wait. This is priority. It began during the pandemic when everyone was staying home. These four friends, including my wife, decided to have a conference call every Tuesday at 10:00. It's coffee and conversation for about two hours, just not at a coffee shop. There is no agenda. They call to keep in touch. They call because they are friends.

You don't get a say in relatives, but a friend is your responsibility. You decide. Then one day you realize that this friend you thought you had chosen is really a gift from God.

I have been blessed since childhood, through my years in school, and as a pastor living in different communities, to have friends. I remember when Vivian and I moved into a parsonage in a small town in Nebraska, my first call as a pastor. Someone told us that we should not have friends. Something about being the pastor for all the people in the congregation. Well, we just ignored that advice and have never regretted doing so.

Muhammad Ali once said, "Friendship is the hardest thing in the world to explain. It's not something you learn in school. But if you haven't learned the meaning of friendship, you really haven't learned anything."

This is from Henri Nouwen, in his book, *Out of Solitude: Meditations on the Christian Life*:

> "When we honestly ask ourselves which persons in our lives mean the most to us, we often find that it is those who, instead of giving advice, solutions, or cures, have chosen rather to share our pain and touch our wounds with a warm and tender hand. The friend who can be silent with us in a moment of

despair or confusion, who can stay with us in an hour of grief and bereavement, who can tolerate not knowing, not curing, not healing and face with us the reality of our powerlessness, that is a friend who cares."

And let's not forget the wisdom of Aristotle, who said, "What is a friend? A single soul dwelling in two bodies."

I have attained the age where losing friends is all too common, and I wonder if they knew how much their friendship meant to me. Did I ever tell them?

So I write these words for myself. Part confession. Part resolve. In the Church we call that repentance. I can do better.

A few years ago, I wrote the following words:

> She's my friend.
> I can tell her everything,
> even the bad things,
> and she still loves me.
> She's my friend.
> I know her almost as well as I know myself.
> I can tell when she is sad or angry or confused by life.
> She's my friend.
> I don't judge her.
> I don't put her down.
> I don't laugh at her;
> I laugh with her.
> She's my friend.
> We can talk for hours and not get tired of the other's voice.
> We can disagree but we don't fight.
> We hear what the other is saying and we understand.
> She's my friend.
> We have each other's back.

> We don't put each other down.
> We don't judge each other's habits.
> We don't name each other's faults.
> She's my friend.
> We trust one another.
> We laugh together.
> We cry together.
> She's my friend.
> When one of us dies, the other will stay near until the end
> and then will weep and remember
> and be glad that she was and always will be ...
> My friend.

I realize that is not terribly profound, but I wrote it to remind myself — and maybe you — to not take your friend or friends for granted. Take time to let your friends know they have blessed you, and that they have kept you.

If these words remind you to keep in touch with an old friend or say a word of thanks to another for being your friend, that will make me feel pretty good.

And when we sing *What a Friend We Have in Jesus*, know that is high praise to Jesus.

I Should Thank Them

She's the gal who greets me
at the deli counter,
whose husband died last summer.
She's the mother who cuts my hair,
while I look at her sons' pictures taped to the mirror.
He's the guy at the post office who sells the stamps,
weighs the packages, and thanks me for coming.
She's the woman at the library
who checks out the books.
She's the lady who runs my credit card
after I fill the car with gas.
We have no connection,
except this brief time.
But I look forward to seeing them,
sharing brief conversation.
We talk about the weather
and about the work. I ask about the kids
and about the cancer.
Since we are almost strangers,
we are safe with one another.
We have other lives in other places:
Spouses, children, loss, joy, struggle, pleasure.
But here, now, there is only welcome and kindness.
Here we let the rest go for this brief fine moment.
I should thank them.

And the Word became flesh and lived among us …
John 1:14

And the Word Became Flesh and Lived Among Us, and We Have Seen His Glory

God became flesh in one human being named Jesus of Nazareth. But we catch glimpses of God and receive God's grace daily as we encounter God's other children. We, too, can be "little Christs" in this world as we intentionally live out our faith by showing God's kindness and love to others. For sure we encounter God in worship, in scripture and prayer, but we also bump into God in the ordinary moments of each day. Because God became flesh and lived among us.

Ready or Not, Christmas Comes

People often ask me, "Are you ready for Christmas?" My stock answer is that it doesn't make any difference because it will come anyway. Even if I have not shopped or wrapped any gifts, even if I am not jolly or in good cheer, Christmas comes.

Mary did not plan to be pregnant. She was not ready for God's messenger to show up, but Gabriel appeared anyway and said, "Hello Mary. God likes you." Mary was nervous and suspicious. Gabriel said again, "God likes you a lot. And, by the way, you're pregnant."

Then the shepherds. They were simply doing what shepherds do. They were not particularly religious or educated. Contrary to our romantic notions, shepherds were mostly poor and smelly. They were not high on the ladder of success, not the kind of guy a father wants his daughter to bring home. But God's messenger came to them anyway, scaring them half to death. And then they did what a shepherd is not hired to do: They left the sheep to look for a baby.

Ready or not, God comes. Prepared or not, God comes. Believing or not, God comes. Ready or not, Christmas comes.

When your spouse, whom you hurt deeply, says through tears, I forgive you, and you know it is true, then know that Christmas comes. When you put some money in an envelope and mark it for the hungry, know that Christmas comes. When you sit by a friend who has lost someone, and you hold their hand, Christmas comes. When you welcome the children, Christmas comes. When you gather in a community of faith, to sing of God's love and to pray, Christmas comes. When hope is gone and you find it hard to believe anymore, and a friend holds you and whispers "God bless you," Christmas comes.

To think we can stop Jesus from coming is to not grasp God's love for this world. Jesus came to that little town of Bethlehem. Jesus still comes into our lives every day.

Laughing Children, Lazy Bears and Singing Snowmen

We put them to bed in early January and they sleep until late November, just after Thanksgiving. Then we go from one to the other and awaken them. They seem pleased to see us, as we are to see them once again.

They are awake and perhaps so are we. Awake to song and laughter and joyous expectation of the days to come. And, of course, the sharing of gifts.

We take them out of their boxes and wrappings and bring them to where they will live for the next several weeks. Charlie Brown and the rest of the Peanuts gang spend their time on a snow-covered wagon, skating, while nearby four children are roasting marshmallows. Charlie and the gang are also on a countertop decorating a doghouse and in Vivian's office singing Christmas carols.

At least a dozen Santa Clauses, all short and wide, look out upon the world from the top of a tall cabinet, while nearby on our old kitchen cupboard some bears are standing around doing nothing. On the kitchen countertop, five children are laughing and baking and eating cookies, assisted by two small bears. And on a corner cabinet stand a family of four carolers, singing whatever Christmas song happens to be in your head.

Angels stand watch at various places, solemn and attentive. Except for the two on our fireplace mantel who are kissing. A snowman with a silly grin sits on a rocking chair in our bedroom, while on our bed lies a young bear wearing a red scarf. But only during the day. At night he moves to a chair.

They are not real, you might say. And you are right. Yet, there is life in them. For they are full of memories of Christmases past, of family and friends who have gifted us with their presence and their love. The smiling snowman, the solemn angels, the laughing children, the singing family, all remind us of love and goodness and joy. So, you see, they are real to us.

And what is real?

In the book of Genesis, when God finished creation He declared it good. Very good, God said, very good.

The Peanuts kids, the short and wide Santas, the lazy bears, the snowmen singing, all tell of love and goodness, of joy and hope. All tell of God's intention, God's hope for this world. A world full of good. That's the real world.

When you say a kind word to another, write a check to help the poor, visit someone who is alone, encourage a child who is having problems, forgive someone who has hurt you, send a note to someone who needs a word of encouragement, that's real.

Because that is the world God created. That is the world God intends. That is the world Jesus came to show us. A world where people take care of one another, where joy and laughter are common, where hope abounds. That's the real world.

That one baby born in a barn in a town called Bethlehem was given to this world to show us what it is like to be real, to be a real human being. So for the last fifty some years, on the day after Thanksgiving, we still go from one to another, open the box, remove the wrapping and awaken them so they can remind us once again of that which is good.

So yes, they are real.

On the floor close to our fireplace sit four large interactive snowmen, one with a dog and penguin, another with a dog, a third with two penguins, and one playing a piano. If you push a button, they sing Christmas songs.

When our grandson, Benjamin, was about 4 or 5, riding in the back seat of the car, he was singing *Have a Holly Jolly Christmas*. His grandmother asked him, "Where did you learn that song? In school?" Benjamin replied, "At your house, Grandma." He learned it from a snowman who is not real.

The Peanuts band is right outside our front door, Lucy playing flute, Linus on keyboard, Charlie Brown on sax and Snoopy strumming his guitar. Christmas music. Whatever song you remember, they remember. Whatever song is in your heart, they can play.

His Name is Jesus, and He is Lamb and He is Shepherd

John saw Jesus coming toward him and declared, "Here is the lamb of God who takes away the sin of the world!" John 1:29

When my father left the farm in North Dakota at the age of 37 and moved west to work in a paper mill, he was able to wash the dirt from under his fingernails but never from his soul. For the next 48 years, he kept up with the price of oats and barley and read the Rugby weekly newspaper. When he settled in Washington state, he bought a house in the country, which sat on a hilly 2 ½ acres of land covered with trees, wild grass, blackberry bushes and thistles. My father was constantly at war with those thistles. It was land that would not be farmed, but could sustain a few sheep and a couple of goats for the sake of memory and loss.

I was, at times, the shepherd of those sheep. There was a creek next to our land, at the bottom of the hill on the south side. It was never deep or wide, so if a person — or an animal — could walk across. One day those sheep tried and got stuck in the middle of that muddy creek. I found them that way and knew I had to get them out. I was alone, but with some effort and time, I successfully herded them back to dry land.

Later that same day, I went to check on them. They were in the middle of that same creek, stuck in the same muddy spot.

I do not remember if it was that summer or another, but one day I went looking for those sheep and found their bodies in the corner of a fence line. That is where the wild dogs finally caught them and ripped their throats out.

It has been thought that sheep are not intelligent. They do fall below the pig and are on par with the cow in IQ. But they do stick together.

They recognize the faces of other sheep and remember those faces for years. And they recognize the faces of human beings.

So Jesus, the good shepherd, says of his sheep, "I know my own and my own know me." John 10:14

his name is Jesus
and he is lamb
and he is shepherd
sent by God
for he is son
born among us
so God came
this gentle one
he is lamb
and he is shepherd
lamb of God
without spot
nor blemish
yet slaughtered
yet slain
yet dead
lamb of God
now shepherd
of the earth
now prince
of peace
now risen
from the dead
he is lamb
and he is shepherd
searching for the
lost and scattered ones
lost in hunger

lost in fear
lost in sadness
longing for
a shepherd's voice
to hear
he is lamb
and he is shepherd
leading us
with grace filled
words
words of peace
words of justice
words of welcome
he is lamb
and he is shepherd
see him now with
eyes of faith
for still he comforts
still he leads us
hold him close
this lamb of God
follow him still
this good shepherd
we are sheep
and we are shepherds
sometimes lost
and scattered too
yet we seek

to find
the missing
the wounded
the broken
to listen
to heal
to forgive
because we have been
found
and healed
and forgiven
his name is Jesus
and he is lamb
and he is shepherd
and he is good

– 59 –

Five Loaves and Two Fish ... Bringing What We Have

You know the Bible story, told in all four gospels. Jesus. The disciples. A crowd. Supper time. "Send the crowds away so that they may ... buy food for themselves." "They need not go away. You give them something to eat." "All we have here are five loaves and two fish." "Bring them here to me." Jesus takes what they have. The people are fed.

I would suggest it is more than a story. It is an invitation. For sure with different characters in different places, but this gospel story is repeated over and over again.

Here is how the story is told by a Catholic priest, remembering his father.

"My father was a baker. Every day a man we called Old Johnny Donovan would stop by the bakery. John was a bachelor, never did much as far as I could see, just putter around in his garage next to his dilapidated house. Behind our parents' backs we called him a bum. And every day Old John would just happen to drop in at the back of my father's bakery shop at lunch time, and my dad would always say, 'John, we have some leftover buns. Would you stay and have lunch with us?' Old John's standard response was, 'Well Charlie, I've had plenty to eat already, but like yourself, I hate to see good food go to waste.' Then he would stay and have some buns with my dad and share the local gossip."

"Even as a kid I was awed by this daily drama, that they both were conning one another. So one summer day, after John had left, I finally asked my dad why he just didn't come out and say, 'Hello John, looking for a free lunch again.' My father said, 'Well son, it might hurt John's feelings to say that, and then I could begin to think he was in my debt. The poor are their own gift to us, and we owe them.' He said no more."

Matthew's telling of the story begins with these words: "Now when Jesus heard this, he withdrew from there in a boat to a deserted place by himself." What had Jesus heard?

It was news of the execution of John the Baptist, his cousin, the man who baptized him, who was, in a way, Jesus' pastor. His pastor had been killed. Jesus was in mourning, a wounded healer, one who understands what it is to need compassion.

Jesus is in charge. The disciples obey. They know it won't work, but they obey. That's all Jesus asks of them. And us.

When I was working as a pastor, I would get calls in the middle of the night. Someone was in the hospital, and I was asked to come. I would thank the person at the other end of the line, but I was not always thankful. It was 3 in the morning. It was dark. It was winter. But I would slide out of bed, plant my feet, put on my clothes and go out the door. Not because I felt like it or because of my great compassion. It was hard to have compassion at 3 in the morning, but one is still able to obey. Jesus has compassion. I was simply obeying an order. "You give them something to eat." "Bring what you have to me."

Jesus does not tell the disciples that they must have more compassion, more faith, that they must pray about it. He tells them to simply bring what you have. Let's feed these people.

I am guessing all of us have said from time to time, "Oh, how I wish I had a lot of money. I would do some good. If I only had the ability, the talent."

Jesus says to bring what you already have. Not what you wish you had, or what you hope someday to bring, but what God has already blessed you with.

Elizabeth Eaton, the Presiding Bishop of the Evangelical Lutheran

Church in America, wrote: "... no matter how bleak a congregation's circumstances seem to be, there already exists some capacity in that congregation for mission and ministry. We are not helpless people .... God has already given us what we need to participate with God in the work of God's kingdom. Too often we lapse into a paralysis of grief or anxiety or nostalgia that renders us incapable of seeing anything but scarcity."

Jesus fed those people not because they were nice to him or because they were hardworking, or because they deserved it. He fed them because they were hungry, just so he healed people because they were sick.

One translation of the story concludes with, "And all ate and were satisfied." All were satisfied. Jesus is tickled. The disciples are giddy. The crowd is full. All were satisfied. Because Jesus is obeyed. Because the disciples bring what they have.

Always, always, there is a great crowd of people in need, so many as to overwhelm us and the temptation is to do nothing. "Send the crowds away ...." "We have nothing here but five loaves and two fish."

A guy goes to his neighbor and asks to borrow his ax. The neighbor says, "Sorry, I can't let you have it. I must use it to shave." The man says, "That's a silly excuse," and the neighbor replies, "When you don't want to do something, one excuse is as good as another."

I can hear the disciples, one saying, "We have nothing here," and then another disciple chimes in, "Well, that's not strictly true. We do have five loaves." Then another pipes up. "We also have two fish." At first they have nothing, and then they take inventory and find that they do have something. It's not as much as they would like, but something.

Jesus says, "Bring what you have to me."

Seven Words of Jesus From the Cross

Word One   Luke 23:34
"Father, forgive them for they know not what they are doing."

She jumped off the cliff
And cursed gravity.

We know what we are doing,
But we don't know what we are doing.

He cheats on his wife.
He knows what he is doing,
But he doesn't know what he is doing.

She slaps her child in the face.
She knows what she is doing,
But she doesn't know what she is doing.

Word Two   Luke 23:43
"Truly I tell you, today, you will be with me in paradise."

It is not that God won't forget you.
God remembers you.

The thief is forgettable.
No one records his name.
He is simply one of two criminals.

We do not know his crime.
We do not know his age, gender, color.
Did he have a family?
Did he leave behind a wife and children?
Did his parents watch him die?

This we know:
He believed he was condemned justly.
He believed he deserved to be punished.

He believed that Jesus was innocent.
He believed Jesus could remember him.

So he asked,
With nothing to lose.
A desperate plea for help.
Hope beyond hope.

What if there is no kingdom?
What if there is nothing beyond this moment?
And I am dying?
Then nothing but nothing but nothing?

We have only a word.
We have only faith.

Word Three   John 19:26
"Woman, here is your son. Here is your mother."

THEN
Sing Mary, of your child yet unborn,
Silently in your room.
Sing Mary, childbearing child,
Quietly to the groom.

Sing terror to the deaf stone speaking,
Warning to the throne.
Sing empty all the sweet glass breaking,
Homeless to the crown.

Sing hope to naked feet walking,
Melody to the bread.
Sing full all the masses whispering,
Banquet to the band.

THEN
Sing Mary, of the child yet unborn,
Silently in your heart.
Sing Mary, afraid dear mother,
Quietly now the start.

THEN
Sing joy to the bride and groom,
Come to the wedding dine.
Sing laughter from the sad hearts turn,
Changing water into wine.

NOW
Sing Mary, wail and rage and fear,
Nothing now to give.
Sing Mary, this child you carried,
Too dangerous to live.

NOW AND THEN
My how he loves you Mother Mary,
With final breath,
No words of love for world now.
No need.
He sees you Mother Mary,
He cares for you, provides for you,
Keeps you safe, protected, watched over.

The world must follow.

We know the love of God in small pieces.
By seeing those pieces, we know something of the whole.

Hear the love of the Lord Jesus for Mother Mary,
and so hear God's love for you.

Comfort for Mary.

Mary, surprised by God,
chosen by God.

Mary, hiding in her heart
the truth of her son.

Mary, filled with pride,
yet knowing she will not keep him.

Mary, watching murder,
so very, very helpless.

Then comfort for Mary.
Now comfort for you.

God is great enough to love the whole world,
and greater still to love each one.

This one,
born of Mary,
Son of God,
hears you when you pray.

Word Four   John 19:28
"I am thirsty."
Pain,
A cry,
Tears.
A slippery weight of flesh
And God appears.

A baby.
A body.

Shepherds breathed on him,
Tickled his toes.

Mary held him to her breast,
Wiped his nose.

Jesus crawled on his knees,
Took his first steps,
Stumbled,
Fell,
Ran.

Not mist,
Not ghost,
Nor figment.

But man.
A body.

Word Five   Matthew 28:46 and Mark 15:34
"My God, my God, why have you forsaken me?"

Happy Lent!
So the letter ended.

Happy Lent.
The words don't fit.
Happy suffering.
Happy dying.
Happy death.

Dare we suggest
That the Church may be sad?
That Jesus did not know of Easter?
That He too lived by faith?

Word Six   John 19:30
"It is finished."

We were in the pew together.
Dad, daughter, mom.

I'm the dad.

In the midst of the music,
I begin to cough.
Mom handed dad a remedy,
In a child-proof container.

In a dad-proof container.

My daughter, between,
Took it from my helpless hand,
With quick twist,
Smile and pride,
Handed me the open jar.

I am in good hands,
My future is secure.

In that good moment, I realized my daughter's love and care for me. When need be, she will watch over me, and she will do for me what I am unable to do for myself.

We say, Jesus died for me. What does that mean?

Part of what it means is that you are in good hands, your future is secure.

In the great mystery of Jesus dying on a cross something happened for you. It was not simply one more violent death of another good person.

Word Seven   Luke 23:46
"Father, into your hands I commit my spirit."

I keep saying I am middle aged.
If that be so, I will live to be 150

Time is not spent.

It runs out like sand
From a sack with a hole,
And the hole keeps getting bigger.
I have found nothing to patch the hole.

I like this world.

I like getting up early,
Sitting at the kitchen counter,
Eating toast and reading the paper.

I like the touch of my wife's hand
As we walk silently down the road.

I like the taste of apple and cheese.

I like to laugh,
Talk to children,
Take a nap after lunch,
Read a book,
Listen to music,
Wake up in the morning.

I like this world.
Am I too much in love with this world?
I have come to trust what I know,
And what I know has been good to me.

My Lord loved this world,
Even when the world turned against him.
But my Lord trusted our Heavenly Father.
He knew to whom he belonged.

The Sabbath is Over

Business as usual.
"Fishing," says Cephas.
The sun comes up,
The men hide away.
The women go out
To visit the cemetery.
The stone.
"Who will move the stone?"
Death is a large stone.
Prejudice,
Guilt,
Anger,
Shame,
War,
Discrimination.
Many large stones.
So life won't get out.
You must go to the tomb
To see why churches are built.
Then look up.
The stone has been moved.
Where is Jesus?
"Fishing," says Peter,
"For life."

Doubt and Fear

"So they ... fled from the tomb, ... and they said nothing to anyone, for they were afraid."

Those are perhaps the first recorded words about Easter, found in the gospel of Mark.

The first response to the possibility that Jesus was alive was fear.

According to Luke, when the women tell the eleven disciples about the empty tomb, "these words seemed to them an idle tale, and they did not believe them."

In John's telling, Jesus appears to ten of the remaining eleven disciples. Later, when they tell Thomas they have seen Jesus alive, he replies, "I doubt it."

Easter, the most important and oldest festival of the Christian Church, is rooted in this most unbelievable story that is first greeted with fear and doubt.

It was a quiet, ordinary morning. No magnificent sunrise. No angel choir. No booming voice from heaven. Only the faithful women, the empty tomb and a messenger saying simply, "He has been raised. Go tell."

The women were afraid, of course. And those first disciples doubted. But they did tell. Perhaps they were still afraid, and perhaps they doubted, but they did tell.

And the telling has come down through the years, from parent to child, friend to neighbor, stranger to stranger, and we who have heard the telling have believed, even in the midst of our unbelief and our fears. And we tell.

In our coming together to worship, we tell. With our lives, striving to follow his path and do his will, we tell. With our words, speaking hope, and with our silence, listening with compassion, we tell. We tell the story of Easter, the story of Jesus and God's love.

But Some Doubted

In Matthew's telling of the Easter story, two Marys come to the cemetery to stand before the grave of Jesus. When they arrive, they are met by an angel, a messenger of God, sitting on the large stone that had recently covered the cave grave. This messenger tells the two women to not be afraid, which is like telling the wind in South Dakota not to blow. For sure they are afraid.

The messenger then tells the women that he (or she) knows they are looking for Jesus, but they won't find him in his grave. "He is not here, for he has been raised." They are told to go tell the other followers that Jesus has been raised from the dead and he will meet them in Galilee.

The women leave the cemetery "quickly with fear and great joy," and hurry to tell the others, but before they get very far, they run into Jesus. He tells them, once again, to not be afraid and to go tell the others that he will meet them in Galilee.

Galilee is a region, so it is not like telling someone I will meet you at the corner of East Kemp and North Broadway. But his followers seem to know, and so Jesus is once again with his closest friends, and Matthew writes these remarkable words.

"When they saw him, they worshipped him, but some doubted."

Well of course they did. Matthew doesn't tell us who doubted or how many, but these are the eleven, his closest friends. They spent three years together. They saw him arrested. Some watched him die.

Whoever they were, I like them. No self-righteousness. No arrogance. No pretending. There is an honesty here that is refreshing. Some doubted.

I can relate to that.

Thomas Came to Church

Thomas came to church
the Sunday after Easter
and Jesus was there.
To his amazement,
Thomas discovered
he did not
need to touch Jesus.
Presence was sufficient.
Word was grace.
Faith was enough.

Running

Mary ran from the tomb,
from the terror.
She ran to find Simon and Peter.
She ran to tell.
Then
Simon and Peter
run back to the tomb.
They run to find someone
they hope is not there.

Easter

Easter is not about spring.
Not about new grass appearing.
Not about the warm air,
the lengthening of days.
Not about a fresh start,
or taking a walk in the park
to hear the birds sing.
One must go to the cemetery,
read the names on the stones,
bring to mind the sound of his voice,
see her eyes smiling once again.
Memories and tears.
Only memories and tears.
Then listen, listen,
hear the story once again.

Morning Benediction

It was early when
I stepped into Hardee's
to pick up breakfast.
He looked tired already.
Perhaps because of the time.
Perhaps because of the job.
His voice carried no emotion.
Take your order?
For here or to go?
Routine.
Said it too often already.
I stepped to the counter.
Take your order?
For here or to go?
I handed him my credit card.
He swiped it, looked at it.
Thank you Gary Westgard.
I looked at his name tag.
Thank you Charlie.
I backed away, waited.
My order came.
Leaving,
I shouted across the room.
Hey Charlie!
He looked up.
Have a good day.
He smiled.
Almost at the door,
he shouted back to me.
Thank you.
Then added with
that smile now in his voice.
God bless.

— 75 —

What Does it Mean

O tell me,
What does it mean
To live, to live
In the covenant God made,
To live, to live
In the promise God made
The day you were born
By water, by Word.
To live, to live
In the promise God made,
In the covenant made.
What does it mean
To live.
O tell me.

1. It means living among God's curious clan,
   Sharing pain, tears, delight,
   Giving sign to God's faith and plan;
   Silent speech, a warming light.

2. It means listening for God's wandering Word
   From printed page and preacher.
   Gathered with folk who have heard,
   Inviting all to the Galilean teacher.

3. It means being hungry and being fed,
   Meeting round the welcome board.
   A sip of wine, a bit of bread;
   Servant food from the crucified Lord.

4. It means speaking forgiveness, telling truth;
   Words creating life, shouting glory.
   Loosening tongues of women, men, youth;
   Setting free the incarnate story.

5. It means giving people holy worth,
   Seeing the child, hearing the poor,
   Kneeling before a tired, bloody earth;
   Outstretched hands, an open door.

6. It means building safe sanctuaries,
   Making places of forever peace:
   Playgrounds, churches, schools, librarians;
   Living God's will, making wars cease.

This Wonderful, Wonderful Gift

I have discovered that when I am washing dishes I can take a pan or a dish on which food has dried hard, and I can scrub and scrub and scrub. Or I can place the dish or pan in hot soapy water, walk away for a while and let it soak. When I come back in a few minutes, the water has done its work. I am pretty sure this is not a new discovery.

Perhaps God realized the same thing. So God gave us baptism. God lets the water do its work.

"I have been baptized." That was Martin Luther's response when asked, "How do you know you are a Christian?"

"I have been baptized."

Now we might wonder, where does faith come in? Does one not have to believe? I think Luther was saying that we need solid ground on which to stand, a firm foundation. Faith can be a rather fragile, unsteady thing.

Our prayers don't get answered as we would like. Troubles come, and it is hard to believe in this good God. Then there are times we may doubt God could love us because we do stupid things, speak hurtful words to those we love, turn our backs on the hungry and the poor. So we may wonder, am I really a follower of Jesus? Does God love me? Can God love me?

How do you know you are still a Christian? Luther said, "I have been baptized."

Jesus was baptized. He said it was necessary. I think it was necessary, in part, because of his desire to be as we are, to be one with us, even in baptism.

Jesus' ministry began with his baptism. I believe the same can be said of you and me. By virtue of our baptism, you and I have a ministry. My ministry may not look like yours, just like hands don't do the work of feet, yet each one is essential for the work of the whole body.

We went to a McDonald's. We had a gift card and a coupon, so we asked the young woman at the counter, if it would be better to use a coupon or go for their special that day. It took a few minutes. Afterward I thanked her, said she was good at what she did. She had waited upon us with knowledge and patience and kindness. She had a ministry.

The guy who drives the bus. The gal who cuts your hair. The teacher at school. The family that farms the land. The doctor who brings healing. The guy who fixes your car. The crew that plows the street. The nurse, the electrician, the plumber, the waitress ... they all do ministry.

You do ministry. You have been baptized and you have a ministry.

And if there is a day when you doubt God's care for you, and you wonder if you really are a Christian, you can say with Martin Luther, "I have been baptized."

God will save without baptism, because baptism is for our sake, not for God's. Baptism is God's gift to us, not our gift to God. Baptism is for our good, not because God needs such an offering. God holds us to baptism. We do not hold God to baptism. Baptism is one of God's most visible and precious gifts. It is so simple: a splash of water and a few words. But perhaps most of the beautiful and gracious gifts in this world are the plain and simple ones.

I baptized a man who was 101. He, of course, did not remember his baptism, was never told he was baptized, had no written record of his baptism, so he asked if I would baptize him just to make sure, because he wanted to be baptized.

I baptized Britany, who was born premature. The doctors thought she might not live very long. Shortly after she was born, I reached into the glass incubator that held her tiny body and used an eye dropper filled with water. Easter Sunday. A few years back I attended her wedding.

I baptized my two grandsons, Benjamin and Samuel, both at Joy Ranch, just outside of Watertown. When Benjamin was baptized, it was Christmas and we worshipped in the old country church that sits nearby. There was no running water, so I asked Vivian to bring water and to make it hot, because it was a cold winter day. As we prepared for baptism, I poured the water into the font. As the steam rose, I tested the water and found it too hot. I explained that to the congregation. A gentleman in the pew got up, went outside and came back with a handful of snow, which he placed in the water to cool it. He was farmer. Farmers have a knack of making up stuff when such help is needed. It was needed and it worked. We proceeded with the baptism.

Baptism is a holy thing, but also a very human thing. It's an old man wanting to make sure. It's using an eye dropper in a hospital room. It's being washed with South Dakota snow.

A good pastor from another denomination once said to me, "You Lutherans make too much of baptism." I don't remember answering him, but I disagree. I think we do not make enough of baptism. It is precious gift. And it is always that, a gift. Whether the one baptized is a few hours old or 101 years old, it is always a gift. A wonderful gift.

Martin Luther also said this: "When you wash your face, remember your baptism."

What Does Jesus Have to Say?

True story. He is a lawyer, a good one, who has argued before the Supreme Court. There was a time when he stood before that Court on behalf of those who wished to uphold California's ban on gay marriage. He supported the ban. While making arguments in the case, he learned that one of his children is gay. Later he found himself helping his daughter plan her wedding with another woman. In other words, he changed his mind.

Another true story. A United States senator, who was on record as opposed to gay marriage, also changed his mind when his son announced he was a gay man. The senator said, "It allowed me to think of this issue from a new perspective, and that's of a dad who loves his son a lot and wants him to have the same opportunities that his brother and sister would have, to have a relationship like Jane and I have had for over 26 years."

In the Christian church when you change your mind it is called repentance.

I am glad these gentlemen love their children enough to see with new eyes, are willing to change their minds, willing to repent, and willing to say so out loud.

What makes me sad, a bit angry, is that these two men were not able to see that everyone who is gay is someone's son or daughter. These men changed their minds only when they looked into the eyes of their own children. They failed to look into the eyes of other people's children.

We share this earth with a great variety of people. I remember in Sunday School singing, "Red, brown, yellow, black and white, they are precious in his sight. Jesus loves the little children of the world."

When God completed creation, "God saw everything that God had made, and indeed, it was very good" (Genesis 1:31). In truth, some of God's children are gay. They are born that way. And they are loved by God. Shame on us when we make others feel guilty or less or ashamed for who they are.

About this time, some of you reading these words are getting more than a bit upset with me. You will tell me to read my Bible. Fair enough. But then let us also ask some questions of the Bible.

Pastor David Lose, former professor at Luther Seminary in St. Paul and former president of Lutheran Seminary in Philadelphia, asks, "What does the Bible really say about homosexuality?" Here is a part of his answer:

"Actually, a whole lot less than you might imagine! That may be hard to believe given the fierce rhetoric Christians often employ when talking about homosexuality, but there are really only seven passages in the Bible that refer directly to homosexual behavior, and none of them are associated with Jesus. Compare that to the more than 250 verses on the proper use of wealth or more than 300 on our responsibility to care for the poor and work for justice, and you appreciate quickly that homosexuality was not exactly a major theme of the Bible." (Huffington Post, Oct. 10, 2011)

Leviticus (chapters 18 and 20) does include verses that speak of homosexual behavior as an abomination. But Leviticus (chapter 19) also gives instruction on how men should cut their hair and commands that no one get a tattoo. So what does one do with this book? Do the words of Leviticus finally guide us in faith and life?

The Apostle Paul, in letters to the Christian congregations in Rome (Romans 1:26-27) and Corinth (I Corinthians 6:9-11), and to his friend Timothy (I Timothy 1:9-11), wrote words of judgment upon homosexual behavior. But the passages raise the question of whether Paul was speaking of consensual, loving, committed relationships or was he speaking of rape?

I am a Christian who leans Lutheran. The Apostle Paul is important to me. "Justification by grace through faith" is a central tenant of our Church. But I don't agree with everything Paul says. Writing to the congregation in Corinth, Paul concludes "… in all the churches of the saints, women should be silent in the churches … should be subordinate …" (I Corinthians 14).

Paul lived in a different time. I believe today he would come to a different conclusion about the participation of women in the Church. In the same way, today we have a better understanding about what it means to be gay, that being gay is not a matter of choice, but a matter of birth.

What kind of life do I want to lead? More importantly, who do I want to follow?

I do not wish to live my life making judgments upon others. God will judge us all, and as Frederick Buechner writes in *Listening to Your Life*, "the one who judges us most finally will be the one who loves us most fully."

It is much more fun to live a life of welcome, seeing each person as a child of God, an heir to the kingdom of heaven, and enjoying their company while we share this earth for a brief time.

Finally, the writer of Leviticus is not Jesus. Moses is not Jesus. Paul is not Jesus. And I have decided to follow Jesus.

So then, what does Jesus have to say about homosexuality? Absolutely nothing.

Let love be genuine; hate what is evil, hold fast to what is good.
Romans 12:9

The Quiet Season

We have been in the quiet season
for quite some time now.
There is the sound of machines:
cars and pickups, snowmobiles
roaring through the park,
snowplows moving too quickly,
as if they had done something wrong.
Once in a while a dog barks,
pleading to be let inside.
But no sound of leaves or birds.
What is missing most is
the sound of the human voice.
My neighbor is out walking his dog,
but they have been together now
for quite some time and
feel no need for conversation.
Construction workers are
observed from inside my car,
but my windows are shut.
Then yesterday the boys
from next door came out.
The snow now is old and dirty,
but the boys don't care.
They are outside once again.
Their talk and their laughter
is a promise.
I heard spring yesterday.

Grandmother

Like a great oak tree,
Under whose branches you sat
In your morning sun.
Whispered wisdom blowing gently,
Sturdy, dependable,
Like the changing seasons.
In the spring rain
And summer heat
You grew from child to woman.
In the colors and changes of fall
You grew strong.
In her winter
Patient wisdom was born.
To rest back once more on her strength
And to speak your heart.
To play again on her branches.
An afternoon perhaps.
Oh how lovely, how kind.
But only memory,
And tears,
And thanksgiving,
And God.

One of a Kind

The world doesn't need another
person like myself,
he said.
One of me
is quite enough.
But I see with
different eyes.
For when he is gone,
there will be no other.
So I best pay attention to
this one. This unique
creation.
No one like him,
before or after.
A fine and precious
jewel,
made by
the hand of God.
One of a kind.

Getting Ready for the Day

As God's chosen ones, holy and beloved, clothe yourselves with compassion, kindness, humility, meekness, and patience. Above all, clothe yourselves with love, which binds everything together in perfect harmony. And let the peace of Christ rule in your hearts, to which indeed you were called in the one body. And be thankful. — Colossians 3:12, 14-15

The apostle Paul is thought to have written these words, but hear them now as if they are being spoken by your mother. It is morning, and you are going out for the day, whether to work or play, and she is telling you what you should wear.

Time to get ready,
she says, with a smile,
time to be out in the world
for a while.
You must dress for the day,
put on your best.
Let me look at you now,
let me see what you chose.
Ah, yes, compassion, good choice,
and kindness for sure.
But don't leave your patience
here by the door.

Humility and meekness
may seem out of style,
but give them a try,
put them on for a while.
Don't forget your coat,
it can get cold out there.
So put on love, warm love,
let the world know you care.
You can't know the weather,
but you have peace in your soul,
you are dressed in God's grace,
so be thankful, be bold.

Consider the Power of Words

Vivian and I recently went to a local store. There is a road that runs in front of the store and a crosswalk that leads from the front door across the road into the parking lot.

A couple of people came out of the store and stepped onto the crosswalk. Another couple were coming to the store and so the four of them stopped to visit on the crosswalk. A truck came to the crosswalk and the driver honked his horn several times. One of the standing men yelled at the man in the truck, who then yelled back. The voices were loud, the language foul. In just a few seconds the air was polluted by what came out of the mouths of two grown men. Or maybe they were two adolescent boys who just looked like men.

But it did not have to happen. The guy in the truck did not have to honk. The guy on the street could have easily apologized and stepped back onto the sidewalk. They both chose to do otherwise. They decided to use words to take away life, rather than to give life. Here is another story told by a woman named Mary Ann Bird.

"I grew up knowing I was different and I hated it. I was born with a cleft palate and when I started school my classmates made it clear to me how I must look to others. A little girl with a misshapen lip, crooked nose, lopsided teeth and garbled speech. When they would ask what happened to your lip, I'd tell them I had fallen and cut it on a piece of glass. Somehow it seemed more acceptable to have suffered an accident than to have been born different. I was convinced no one outside of my family could love me.

"There was, however, a teacher, Mrs. Leonard, in second grade, we all adored. She was short, round, happy, a sparkling lady. Annually we would have a hearing test. I was virtually deaf in one ear. But I had discovered when I had taken the test before that if I did not press my hand as tightly upon my ears as I was told to do, I could pass the test.

"We stood against the door and covered one ear. The teacher, sitting at her desk, would whisper something and we would repeat it back. Things like, the sky is blue or do you have new shoes?

"I waited and then heard the seven words which changed my life. Mrs. Leonard said in a whisper, 'I wish you were my little girl.'"

It was only one sentence. Seven words. But they gave life. Words count. Words make a difference. Words matter. You know this to be true because you have been healed by words and you have been wounded by words. We all have.

We read in Genesis that God brought this world into being with a word. "Then God said, 'Let there be light'; and there was light." "God said, 'Let us make humankind in our image, according to our likeness ….'" "So God created humankind in his image, in the image of God he created them …" (Genesis 1). God spoke and there was life. Life giving words. We are created in the image of God, each and every one of us, and we have the power to create life with words. Just so we have the power to bring death with words.

Jesus says, it is not what goes into the mouth, but what comes out of the mouth that defiles (pollutes) a person. (Matthew 15:11)

One more story.

A father is having a conversation with his six-year-old son. The son is upset with his father because he is putting the son to bed earlier than he wants. The son says, "Daddy, I hate you." The father says, "My son, I am sorry you feel that way, but I love you." The child responds, "Don't say that." The father says, "I am sorry, but it is true, I love you." The son protests, "Don't say that again." The father says, "My child, I love you, whether you like it or not."

A father speaking to his son. God speaking to you. Life giving words.

Coming Back to Congregations I Once Served

As I stand before this gentle house of witnesses, I see
among the familiar, yet changed, faces of long-ago friends,
some new faces, new to these old eyes, and I see
some faces carrying the images of those I knew once upon a time;
newer versions of older models.
But I also see faces not changed, lovely faces,
who, in my mind's eye, will be as they were years ago.
For these are numbered in my faith among that great crowd
of witnesses, who no longer grow old, nor have any need of faith,
for they understand fully as they have been fully understood. The
words we once spoke were small and even trivial.
The laughter came easily. Now those words and that laughter are
precious jewels, and I hold dearly each single small stone. Why do
we not learn that while we search, yea yearn, for the good life, we
are living real life, and too soon it is no more. So I come back,
knowing that I cannot come back, but I can remember. Remember
with tender mercy. And I can hope, yes blessed hope, that God will
put an end to endings, and that heaven will be a place of small talk,
easy laughter, lovely faces, with no known word for goodbye.

The Importance of Death

It is late, the meeting over, others
have left for home, but I want to
stay awhile, on this quiet, cloudless
night, here in the country, sit on
the front steps of this old church,
look across to the cemetery, a few
steps away. Old stones sunk in
the ground. Newer stones where
I have stood. You can't enter this
church without seeing the graves
of all who have come before and
those we had come to love.
Sacred ground. A sign.
Death is not off in some far country.
Helps a preacher tell the truth, helps
the people be a bit more humble, not
so arrogant about their faith.
When you stand over a grave in that
cemetery, you look up and see this
building, where I sit now, where
people gather to sing of hope and
still bless God on hot afternoons
in August, on cold, snow-covered days
in February, before carrying another
grandparent or husband or child out
across the road to that place of stones
and memories. This building too is a
sign. The living are not abandoned in
their grief. We come back here after
the journey, come back to hot dishes,
sandwiches, egg coffee, and pie.
Laughter can be heard.

Glad to Have Such Faith, Glad to Have Such Hope

Brittany was terminally ill with brain cancer. The cancer brought terrible pain and sometimes prevented her from speaking or recognizing her own family. There was no hope of a cure. Doctors had removed as much of the tumor as possible. Two months later it grew back. There was only the promise that it would get worse, and she would eventually die. She and her husband moved to Portland, Oregon. Once there she took a drug that enabled her, in her words, to die on her own terms. Brittany was 29.

She said, "My glioblastoma is going to kill me and that's out of my control. I've discussed with many experts how I would die from it and it's a terrible, terrible way to die. So being able to choose to go with dignity is less terrifying.

"For people to argue against this choice for sick people really seems evil to me. They try to mix it up with suicide and that's really unfair, because there's not a single part of me that wants to die. But I am dying."

I have sat at the bedside of lovely people who embraced life, but who had come to a place where death looked to be a friend. My father came to that place. In my last conversation with him, he said, all I want to do is go to sleep and not wake up. I believe Brittany came to that place.

The article relating Brittany's story includes comments from a Wyoming woman who serves on a legislative committee that handles health issues in her state. "My sense is Wyoming would reject it (doctor-assisted suicide), ... it would just be a flat 'no,' .... That's my personal values as well: we don't get to pick. The big guy upstairs chooses when we go and when we stay."

I am not a big fan of addressing God as the "big guy upstairs," but more than that, I would argue that if one has never been in that place where living offers no hope, no joy, no pleasure, but only pain and loss and eventual death, then one should speak slowly or perhaps not at all.

Does God go about choosing "when we go and when we stay," as the woman from Wyoming states? Does God choose death for us?

When someone dies, especially someone young, we hear words like, "God must have needed another little angel," or, "God chooses only the very best," or "God decided it was her time."

I suggest another way of faith.

The Apostle Paul, in a letter to the congregation at Corinth, writes, "The last enemy to be destroyed is death." I Corinthians 15:26

Is it possible there is a battle going on? A battle between God and the enemy?

When his good friend Lazarus died, Jesus did not comment, "Well, it was his time to go. God's will. Because we all know, the big guy upstairs chooses when we go and when we stay."

No. When his good friend died, Jesus wept. God cried. And we do too. But more. God and God's people do battle against the forces of death: poverty, racism, prejudice, injustice, hunger, cancer, heart disease, diabetes — all that strive to take life away.

Death is the enemy.

A decisive battle took long ago, on a day we now call Good Friday. A young Jewish Rabbi named Jesus was put to death. His body was taken down from a cross and laid in a tomb. It seemed once again that the enemy had won.

But when some women came to the tomb early Sunday morning, he was not to be found. Some, who had been his students, his followers, later said they saw him, talked with him, ate with him, were both surprised and glad at his appearing. They told others. The news has traveled down through the centuries, so we too have heard the tale and are free to tell it.

That long ago Sunday morning changed everything. That Sunday morning is a promise that the enemy will not have the final word. That Sunday morning is a glimpse into our future.

The raising of Lazarus was a prelude to that Sunday morning. In the resurrection of Jesus from death to life, we are promised that we, too, will be raised up. We will be set back on our feet again in another part of God's kingdom, no less beautiful than this place. God's promise. Our hope.

Brittany wanted to live, but what she woke up to each morning was not life. The enemy had already won. She just surrendered early. I will not judge her. Neither should anyone else.
And what about God? God weeps.

One day I will die. As will you. I don't much care for the idea. But it will not be God who takes my life. Death is the enemy. In the end, God will have the final word. Life. The last enemy will be defeated.

It is of faith for sure. But I am glad to have such faith, glad to have such hope.

Celebrating Easter Every Day

She was a high school math teacher trying her best to teach her class a difficult new concept. The students were becoming more and more frustrated. Finally, she said, "Look, put away your books. Take out a sheet of paper and list each of the students in our class. Then write something nice about each one." Over the weekend she took those lists, put the name of each student on a sheet of paper and listed all the nice things that the other students had said about that person. On Monday morning she handed the papers out to each one. It got quiet, but then she heard one student say, "I never knew that anybody thought anything nice about me."

The years passed, students came and went, and eventually there was the class reunion. When those students now gathered around their former teacher, one of them pulled out a ragged piece of paper that had been folded and refolded many times. It was that list from long ago. Another told of keeping that list taped to her mirror, so she saw it every morning. Another said she pasted her list in her wedding album. So it went. That piece of paper kept them, told them when they needed to be told that they had value.

That's an Easter story.

A grandfather invites his three-year-old granddaughter, Rachel, to sit on his lap. She is a sad child, just come in from playing. It has not been fun. The other kids are bigger and she has fallen, so she comes to her grandfather with some bumps and bruises, and some sadness. As she climbs upon his lap, Grandpa asks, "Shall I tell you a story about horses that run fast?" "No," she says. "Shall I tell you a story about puppies?" "No." "Shall I tell you a story about Rachel?" "Yes," she smiles, "yes, tell me a story about Rachel."

Easter is the day to tell the story of Jesus. But it is also a story about you and me. For we, too, come with our bumps and bruises, maybe some sadness in our lives. We need to hear about God's love for us and for those we love, for those who no longer walk this earth with us.

There is, in all of us, a child that needs a hug, and who needs to know that someone cares. Oh, we may speak boldly and bravely about living life fully and how all is right with the world. But the child in all of us is still afraid of the darkness and the unknown, and we still get bumped and bruised along the way. So the child in all of us needs someone to tell us a story in which we are included.

The Easter story does just that.

And we want those we meet along the way to also know Easter, not just after they die. But Easter now, in plain sight.

Like the student said, "I never knew that anybody thought anything nice about me." Until one day, someone told him.

It's an old story. I am guessing I first heard it back in the 1970s, and most likely you have heard it, too. Maybe it is okay to hear it again. I believe it is from a book of essays by Loren Eiseley, who lived from 1907 to 1977. The book is called *The Star Thrower* and the story is simply called "The Starfish Story."

A young man is walking along the ocean and sees a beach on which thousands and thousands of starfish have washed ashore. Further along he sees an old man, walking slowly and stooping often, picking up one starfish after another and tossing each one gently into the ocean. "Why are you throwing starfish into the ocean?" he asks. "Because the sun is up and the tide is going out and if I don't throw them further in they will die." "But, old man, don't you realize there are miles and miles of beach and starfish all along it! You can't possibly save them all, you can't even save one-tenth of them. In fact, even if you work all day, your efforts won't make any difference at all." The old man listened calmly and then bent down to pick up another starfish and threw it into the sea. "You're right, but it makes a difference to this one."

I read stories in the newspaper, watch the news on television and I feel both sad and helpless, so I put the paper down, turn off the television and go about my mostly safe life, because a voice says, "But old man, don't you realize there are miles and miles of beach and starfish all along it. Your efforts won't make any difference at all."

And then Jesus comes along and says, "But remember, you can make a difference to someone." We want Easter for those who have died. We want Easter when we die. We want to proclaim Jesus is risen. We want to sing about heaven. But maybe people need to know about Easter now, in this life, in plain view, every day.

That teacher on one ordinary day gave those students a brief glimpse of the Kingdom of God. I am guessing that God sees more in you than you do. How blessed you are, for you get to practice every day living like Jesus' disciples, living like a citizen of the Kingdom of God, helping to create a better world wherever you are, making a difference to someone, celebrating Easter every day.

A Buddhist, a Muslim, and a Christian Walk Into a Bar

A pub actually, and as I am introducing my Muslim friend to my Buddhist friend, I realize this could be the beginning of several jokes.

But I do not think of Adnan as my Muslim friend or Lawrence as my Buddhist friend. I think of them as my friends, and I am blessed by their friendships.

Recently, while visiting family on the west coast, one of my relatives said she was troubled by a woman who came to a gathering with her head covered. "I could only see her eyes." For some odd reason that simple truth made her afraid. She did not realize that such a head covering is a symbol of the woman's faith, the same way a Christian might wear a cross.

One of my teachers in high school had us read the plays of William Shakespeare. I have forgotten much, but the following words, from *The Merchant of Venice* (Act 3, Scene 1), come back quite often. Shylock, a Jew, has been hurt, humiliated, and wants revenge. He spits out these words in anger.

"I am a Jew. Hath not a Jew eyes? Hath not a Jew hands, organs, dimensions, senses, affections, passions? Fed with the same food, hurt with the same weapons, subject to the same diseases, healed by the same means, warmed and cooled by the same winter and summer as a Christian is? If you prick us, do we not bleed? If you tickle us, do we not laugh? If you poison us, do we not die?"

No matter our color, our faith, our politics, we all bleed red. We all have dreams, hopes, loves and fears, whether one wears a cross on a chain around the neck or a scarf on the head. Yet too often we are afraid because the other does not look like us or talk like us or worship like us.

We were at dinner in a restaurant when I noticed that our waitress had a tattoo from her wrist to her elbow. I have learned it is called a half sleeve. After our meal, I asked her about it. "Is it real?" "Did it hurt?" "What did it cost?" "That much!" She was kind and patient, answered all my questions, and added that someday she would get a full sleeve, from her wrist to her shoulder.

At this point I have no desire whatsoever to get a tattoo, but I have no right to judge her, put her in a category, or think she is less because of a tattoo on her arm. She did not know I am a pastor but volunteered to point out the Bible verse that was included in her tattoo, putting her faith on display for all to see. Who knows, perhaps she is a better witness to the faith than me.

God keeps telling us not to be afraid.

Through the prophets, God says, "Do not fear, for I am with you, do not be afraid, for I am your God." (*Isaiah 41:10*)

And we confess with the Psalmist, "Even though I walk through the valley of the shadow of death, I will fear no evil, for you are with me; your rod and your staff, they comfort me." *(Psalm 23:4)*

The angel says to the shepherds, "Do not be afraid; for see — I am bringing you good news of great joy for all the people: to you is born this day in the city of David a Savior, who is the Messiah, the Lord. This will be a sign for you: you will find a child wrapped in bands of cloth and lying in a manger." (*Luke 2:10-11*)

There are bad people in the world, but most — no matter color or faith or country — are just ordinary people, doing the best they can. Most of the people you meet are just as kind as you, and trying just as hard to do what is right and good.

If we fear one another, then the bad people in this world, who do indeed want to cause harm, will have already won.

The Amazing Grace of the Norwegian Goodbye

When I was a kid, both in North Dakota and Washington, we would have family (aunts, uncles, cousins) come into our home for the evening. We would have supper (we always called it supper) and then the children would play, and the "old" people would sit and talk. When I was a kid, I could not figure out how people could enjoy just sitting and talking.

Finally someone would say, "Well, we better get going. Got to get up early tomorrow, and I am sure you do too." So coats, mittens, scarfs and hats would be retrieved from the bedroom where earlier they had been laid out gently on the bed, and the guests would head for the door. Then Mom and Dad would stand by the door with our visitors and keep talking, maybe for ten or fifteen minutes. We kids had quit playing and my cousins had put on their coats, so we just stood there while our parents talked and talked. When I got older, I began to call this phenomenon the "Norwegian Goodbye."

In truth it was a good thing. Back then I thought it long and boring, but now I realize it was a grace. For it was family, and sometimes friends, taking a little more time to share life before going out into the cold. In their own way they were saying to one another, "I am glad you are a part of my life, and it was really good to spend this time with you."

Death has come often this past year. Both family and friends have left, and I have discovered that, along with the sadness of the person's leaving, there is the added sadness of not having expressed my appreciation for the blessing this person has been to me. I wish I would have thanked this one for walking beside me for a time, for the kindness shown me, for the laughter we shared, for the help given along the way. But I didn't get it done. And now it is too late.

Why do we wait to express our gratitude?

I suppose, in part, because death always surprises. We read about death every day, but most often it visits other families, other friends. Then we get the phone call, hear the knock on the door, or read the evening paper. "If only I had known," we say. "I wish I would have had time to say goodbye."

We tend to leave the important conversation until the end, until we are going out the door. Even Jesus did it. In the gospel of John, chapter 14-16, we read Jesus' "Norwegian Goodbye." He is pretty sure that death is near. He has just had supper with his close friends, so before they go out into the cold, he has this long goodbye. He tells his friends he is going away, but not to be troubled, to continue to have faith in him, that he is "going to prepare a place" for them. He tells them that if they love him, they will continue to do his work in this world. And he tells them that he loves them and that he wants them to love one another. The important stuff.

Mother Teresa once said "Yesterday is gone. Tomorrow has not yet come. We have only today. Let us begin."

You and I have today. There is still time to say the important stuff to the people you love before going out the door and into the cold. We have today. Let us begin.

Certainty

The Christian Church
offers comfort to all.
Except one.
That one is named
certainty.
Jesus once said,
If you were blind,
you would have no sin.
But now that you say, 'We see,'
your sin remains.
Oh, the discomfort of
certainty,
sitting in the midst of
faith.

Questions

Why do we look up
to find God?
Is God in the sky?
Why do we imagine
heaven to be above
and hell below?
Do we not catch a
glimpse of heaven
on this earth?
Seeing a baby's
smile.
Hearing the sound of
joy.
Being held by someone you
love.
For sure it is a broken
world.
Yet God is present.
God's deeds are done.
And even here on earth,
as in heaven,
tears are wiped away.

She Hugged the Grieving

... while Jesus went to the Mount of Olives. Early in the morning he came again to the temple. All the people came to him and he sat down and began to teach them. The scribes and the Pharisees brought a woman who had been caught in adultery; and making her stand before all of them, they said to him, "Teacher, this woman was caught in the very act of committing adultery. Now in the law Moses commanded us to stone such women. Now what do you say?" They said this to test him, so that they might have some charge to bring against him. Jesus bent down and wrote with his finger on the ground. When they kept on questioning him, he straightened up and said to them, "Let anyone among you who is without sin be the first to throw a stone at her." And once again he bent down and wrote on the ground. When they heard it, they went away, one by one, beginning with the elders; and Jesus was left alone with the woman standing before him. Jesus straightened up and said to her, "Woman, where are they? Has no one condemned you?" She said, "No one, sir." And Jesus said, "Neither do I condemn you. Go your way, and from now on do not sin again."

John 8:1-11

They are funeral directors. I was a pastor. The three of us worked together too often. We became friends. When they hired another director to work with them, they hired a woman. I asked them how that was working out. They said at first people were a bit hesitant; this was new, a change. Men were funeral directors. Any women on the staff answered the phone, made coffee, or greeted the guests. Women did not prepare the body, direct the pall bearers, lead the parade of cars out to the cemetery.

But she did all of that very well. And she did more. They said she did something they had never done. She hugged the grieving. On that day long ago, Jesus was not confronted by a committee or a delegation. This was a mob of individuals who have forgotten who they are. It is no longer "I." It is only "we." And "we" have only one motive, one desire … to do another human being harm.

I grew up watching westerns. Now I have already lost some of you. A western is pretty much *Star Wars* with different clothes and a horse instead of a spaceship. In one western movie, a mob (all men, of course) comes to the jail intending to hang the prisoner. The lawman confronts the mob, then begins to name each one, remind each one of his family, his history in the community, his relationship to the lawman. Finally, one man, remembering who he is, leaves. Then another and another, until there is only the one, the leader who has no one following him. The lawman does not prevent violence with more violence. In his own way, with understanding, compassion and words, the lawman hugs each one.

What is Jesus writing in the dirt? I have no idea. But perhaps that is not the point. Writing in the dirt takes time. It is like a recess or maybe a sabbath. The mob takes a rest from their labor. Jesus is giving each one time to think, to consider what he is doing, to see himself and ask, "Is this who I am? What if this were my sister, my daughter?"

Jesus does not gather his followers for battle; he never does. Stopping violence with violence is like the parent who teaches the child not to hit by hitting the child. Rather, like my funeral director friend, or like the lawman in that long forgotten western film, Jesus hugs each one.

I am guessing he learned it from his mother.

And then Jesus tells a joke. "Where are they? I don't see them. Do you see them?" And the woman smiles. "No, I don't see them either."

I like to think they were both laughing. Which, I believe, is one of the benefits of forgiveness.

My Responsibility

Today we ate in a restaurant.
I stopped as we left
to thank the man
who served us.
For that is what he did.
He served.
He did not wait upon us.
He served us.
I told him he was good
at what he did.
I meant it.
Every word.
It is my task,
my responsibility
to make the person
I meet
at that moment
feel good
about who
he or she is.
To be glad to be.
To simply be.

Praise God for Broken Cookies

Vivian baked some wonderful cookies a few days ago. I am not sure that "wonderful" is a way to describe something you eat, but they are wonderful, full of raisins and oatmeal, thin and tasty. It happened that a few stuck to the baking sheet and broke while being moved from sheet to rack.

I asked if I could eat a couple. "Yes," she said. "But eat the broken ones. You can have as many of those as you want."

I thought, "Praise God for broken cookies."

The truth is they may not win any prize at the fair, but those broken cookies taste just as good as the "perfect" ones.

There are these words in the Old Testament that Christians believe describe Jesus: "… he had no form or majesty that we should look at him, nothing in his appearance that we should desire him." (Isaiah 53:2)

But on the inside … as Psalm 34 sings, "O taste and see that the Lord is good." (Psalms 34:8)

What is so appealing to me about Jesus are not the miracles and the healings. What attracts me to him is his humanity, compassion, kindness, and desire to lift others up and show them forgiveness.

The miracles and healings are like that "perfect" cookie that is brought to the state fair and wins the purple ribbon. But the compassion and the kindness are like the broken cookie. For such can be found in any of us. We who know we are broken, who fail often and who get so afraid at times, can truly be like Christ in this world, in our compassion and our kindness, in our desire to lift others up and in our courage to forgive.

When someone asked me for help because he or she had a problem with alcohol, I would ask if I could contact a friend who belonged to Alcoholics Anonymous, someone who understood what it was like to "have a problem with alcohol." One broken child of God helping another broken child of God. Or as D.T. Niles said: "Christianity is one beggar telling another beggar where he found a loaf of bread."

It is almost Christmas. As you celebrate the birth of Jesus, as you gather with family and friends, exchange gifts and sing the old carols, please remember that for some this is a season of tears. A loved one is not present this Christmas. There is not enough money to buy presents this Christmas. He or she will sit at table alone this Christmas.

You and I will not fix it. But we can help. We can figure it out and we can do something … a hug, a word, an unexpected gift, some money, your presence.

Praise God for broken cookies. Praise God for one broken child of God helping another broken child of God. For it is wonderful.

Learning to Speak the Beautiful Sound of Sheer Silence

When I wrote these words, I was beginning week ten after having my right knee was replaced. I have lived a long life without pain. I have had no hard falls, no broken bones, no major surgery (until now) and I have never given birth to a baby. My life has been pretty much pain free. So this is a new thing for me, this pain, this constant ache in my leg.

But rather than tell you about my aches and pains, let's discuss how we talk to one another and how we help one another.

Since my surgery, I began to notice something as I interacted with my caregivers and friends. When I was asked, "How are you doing?" I would respond, "Well, okay, but I still have this pain, like a constant toothache in my leg." Pretty much to a person I would get this response: "It will get better, just give it some time." This was meant well and was probably true, but at the time the future didn't mean much. I was concerned about the present, and in the present I just hurt.

That truth brings to mind all the times I have said pretty much those same words to people I have met along the way who were hurting, to the husband or wife who had just lost a spouse, to the friend diagnosed with cancer, to another recovering from surgery, to still another who recently lost their job. "It will get better. You will be okay."

Well, the reality is we don't know. And even if there is truth in it, when one is in the midst of pain, promises about the future don't mean so much. So I wonder now if there were times when I should have just shut up and listened. No advice. No promise. No fancy words of supposed wisdom. Because the person who is hurting only knows now, the present reality, and the ache of pain or loss. And that person only wants someone to hear and understand. Not advice, and no promise that it will be okay. It might not be.

As I look back, I think about my need to fix things for others with fancy words of advice. It became more about me than the person who was hurting. Instead, perhaps I could have asked, "Is there anything I can do to help?" Perhaps I could have offered, "I am here if you need me." I could have wrapped my arms around the person and said nothing at all. No admonition. No instruction. No promises. Just presence.

Pastors like to fix things, but there are some things we cannot fix. I could be wrong, but maybe — just maybe — we pastors talk too much.

There is a story in I Kings, chapter 19, about the prophet Elijah. He is feeling sorry for himself. He has gotten himself into a jam and fears for his life, so he goes off by himself, sits under a tree and asks God to let him die there. He complains that he is the only person of faith left in the world.

A messenger from God tells the prophet to get up, go to a certain place on a mountain and wait for God to speak. Then we are told that on the mountain there was a great wind, "but the Lord was not in the wind; and after the wind an earthquake, but the Lord was not in the earthquake; and after the earthquake a fire, but the Lord was not in the fire; and after the fire a sound of sheer silence." (I Kings 19:11-12) That is when the prophet hears the voice of God. In the sound of sheer silence.

Company is Coming. Let's Eat.

When Jesus looked up and saw a large crowd coming toward him, Jesus said to Philip, "Where are we to buy bread for these people to eat?" He said this to test him, for he himself knew what he was going to do. Philip answered him, "Six months' wages would not buy enough bread for each of them to get a little." One of his disciples, Andrew, Simon Peter's brother, said to him, "There is a boy here who has five barley loaves and two fish. But what are they among so many people?" Jesus said, "Make the people sit down." Now there was a great deal of grass in the place; so they sat down, about five thousand in all. Then Jesus took the loaves, and when he had given thanks, he distributed them to those who were seated; so also the fish, as much as they wanted. When they were satisfied, he told his disciples, "Gather up the fragments left over, so that nothing may be lost." John 6:5-12

Jesus is sort of like your mom. When company comes, whether expected or not, she feeds them. She will find something in the cupboard. So Jesus says to Phil, "How are we going to feed these people?" Phil says, "I could run to town, but we don't have enough money; do I have to remind you, we have no income?"

Andy comes over, and says, "There's a kid here. He brought his lunch, looks like five small loaves of bread and a couple of fish. He said we could have it, but I'm pretty sure it is not enough."

Jesus says, "Good enough, let's eat."

In whatever way you wish to understand what happens next, know that it is a miracle.

Whether Jesus looks to heaven, says a quiet prayer, touches the meager lunch and the bread and fish are multiplied, or whether Jesus looks into the eyes of the people gathered and they, in turn, look at this kid sharing his lunch and decide they could share their lunch, like some kind of grand potluck.

Either way, it's a miracle.

Whether it's a congregation praying or digging in their pockets for loose change, it's a miracle. When something good happens — the hungry being fed, children being saved, or the story of Jesus being told — it is always a miracle.

This story of feeding the multitude is told six times. It shows up in all four gospels. That must mean something. Could it be that God desires that the hungry be fed?

We might just look around and see that we have five loaves and two fish, and so we can begin. We can do something. We will not limit ourselves by what we do not have. Rather we will give of ourselves because of what we do have. And most of you reading these words have enough. Some of us have a lot.

When our son, Josh, was in grade school, Vivian and I were discussing our finances. We weren't in a panic, but we had bills to pay, and our income sometimes had trouble matching our expenses. It was a small problem, but a problem. Josh, unbeknownst to us, overheard and ran into our bedroom crying, telling us that he would help us out; we just needed to tell him what to do.

A little child shall lead them. "This will be a sign for you. You will find a baby in a manger." There's a kid here with five loaves and two fish, wants to share his lunch.

Jesus will have us understand that he came to be someone other than the miracle worker, the bread king. He came to reveal God's love and God's forgiveness and God's will for God's creation. He came to rule our hearts. He came not to make us gods, but to make us truly human. What is it like to be truly human?

When we hurt someone or do something stupid, we sometimes say, "Well, I'm only human." No, when you help someone, when you do something courageous, something good, then you are only human. Look at Jesus. That is what humanity is meant to be.

Jesus, who has compassion for people he did not even know, who invites them to stay for lunch, who welcomes a child to share what he has, who does not listen to reason, but decides, even when it seems impossible, to go ahead and do something good anyway.

Even if you only have five loaves and two fish.

Glory

Now Jesus took with him Peter and John and James, and went up on the mountain to pray. And while he was praying, the appearance of his face changed, and his clothes became dazzling white. Suddenly they saw two men, Moses and Elijah, talking to him. They appeared in glory…. Now Peter and his companions were weighed down with sleep; but since they had stayed awake, they saw his glory…. Luke 9:28-32

She raises every morning at 6. After chores are done, she goes to work at 8. She gets home at 5. The work is hard. The pay is small. One must wonder why she keeps at it, day after day. But they don't know. They don't understand. In that home is her family, the people she loves most of all. Yes, she leaves them in the morning. You could say she comes down from the mountain. But she returns to them every evening. That family is her glory. It is why she leaves and why she comes back.

There is the little baby who has learned how to clap and she loves it, so she claps over almost everything. Put breakfast in front of her and she claps. Set her in a circle of toys and she claps. Her parents took her to the seashore to watch the waves roll in and she clapped. Her parents say, "We only worry that someday she will stop."

The glory of life. Too soon we lose the habit of applause.

A mother took her young son on a train trip. As they rode across the countryside the boy was so excited he kept jumping up and down, pointing out the window, shouting, "There's a cow! Look Mommy there's a cloud! There are some birds in the tree!"

The mother sensed that perhaps he was disturbing others. "Please forgive my little boy's excitement," she said. "The world is still wonderful to him."

The glory of the flower. The glory of a starlit night. The glory of the rising sun. The glory of the mystery that is life. The glory of a newborn child. The glory of family and friends and faith.

The Gift of Sabbath

We, as Christians, tend to associate Sabbath with worship. But in the beginning God blessed and hallowed the seventh day because on that day God rested. The emphasis was on rest from labor, rest from work completed.

Psalm 145 sings, "Every day I will bless thee, and praise thy name for ever and ever." Worship is not one communal act performed one day out of seven. Worship is a part of who we are as people of faith. It is a part of our work and our play and our rest.

Love of God and love of neighbor are of one piece, so worship is performed when we pay attention to the neighbor in need. Jesus says the first commandment is to love God with all heart, mind, strength. The second commandment is just like the first, we are to love neighbor.

Is it possible that by helping another we are experiencing Sabbath? Or is Sabbath all about rest? Then the question is what constitutes rest? Is rest for one the same as rest for another? Or do we really rest when we watch television, play golf or go sailing? Is rest quitting an obligation to do a joy?

Rest is not defined in Genesis. We are told God completed the task of creation. God quit creating. So rest is not defined as taking a nap. It is defined as being done. God finished the work and God was done (God rested from all the work).

We say we are never done. But maybe we are, for now. So we can rest. We can quit. We will begin again. But for now I quit. I have finished this much work for now. So I rest. I Sabbath.

In the gospels, Jesus is accused of breaking the law by both plucking grain and by healing a man, both done on the Sabbath. In the first case he hearkens back to I Samuel when David, who is hungry, eats bread set aside for worship. In the same way, Jesus says, these disciples need food. Feeding the hungry and healing the sick take precedence over strict adherence to the law.

It goes on to say that Sabbath was made to serve us. We were not made to serve Sabbath. Sabbath is gift, not obligation. We are not slaves to Sabbath. Sabbath is our servant.

But how do I provide or make possible Sabbath for another? How much power do I have to provide Sabbath for others? And if it were possible to close stores on Sunday, would I be helping those workers or would I simply be serving Sabbath? Jesus fed the disciples on Sabbath. Do I take away income (food) from today's disciples by obeying Sabbath. Does then Sabbath serve us or are we serving Sabbath?

We are commanded (obligated) to forgive. It would follow that we are obligated to offer or provide or make possible Sabbath for others. To not make possible Sabbath for others would be a sin, a breaking of the commandment to love neighbor as one loves self. If I need and desire Sabbath for myself, I must therefore desire and provide for Sabbath for others. This is what God has decided; I don't get a vote.

But how do I do that? How do I make possible Sabbath for others?

Something is Wrong and We Seem Unable or Unwilling to Fix it

Melinda Gates once said, "All lives have equal value."

In February of 2014, Tom Brokaw, well respected national news reporter and a South Dakota boy, was diagnosed with multiple myeloma, a cancer affecting blood cells in the bone marrow. In December he announced that the cancer was in remission. "My last year was a challenge," he wrote, "but I was meeting it in world class hospitals with brilliant physicians."

I like Tom Brokaw, and I am glad the cancer is in remission. I'm glad he had "brilliant physicians" in "world class hospitals."

But what if everyone diagnosed with cancer could say the same? What if "the greatest nation in the world" figured out a way to provide health care for all who live in this country?

That is not a political question. It is a faith question.

Jesus, our Good Shepherd, said, "I came that my sheep may have life and have it abundantly." Another translation reads, "... that they have life, and have it to the full." (John 10:10)

So he gave sight to a blind man, caused a deaf man to hear, enabled a leper to go home once again. The task of the Church is not only to announce God's forgiveness and proclaim the promise of heaven. We also work and give and teach in the hope that all God's children have an abundant, full life here on earth.

As the Church, as disciples of Jesus, we will help the neighbor when troubles come. We will send a few bucks to feed the hungry and ship quilts to people we will never meet.

But we will also strive to figure out a way to pay people a decent wage and we will work toward the goal of available quality health care for everyone, regardless of income or status. We will work to stop domestic violence and we will demand that all people be treated with respect.

Will we succeed? Probably not. But shame on us if we don't give it our best shot.

Horace Mann (1796-1859) said, "Be ashamed to die until you have won some victory for humanity."

Jesus came into this world because something is wrong with us. He came to open our eyes to see that truth, and to give us the courage to fix it. In the Bible, God is always telling us not to be afraid. I believe that word is not just about being afraid of what goes bump in the night, but also about not being afraid to do that which is right and good, even when it is hard, or maybe even impossible.

There is a story in the Bible about a man who runs up to Jesus and asks, "What must I do to inherit eternal life?" Jesus asks him if he has kept the commandments of God. The man says, yes, since I was a child. Then, "Jesus, looking at him, loved and said, 'You lack one thing; go, sell what you own, and give the money to the poor …'" Mark 10:17-21

"What must I do?" asks the young man. "What must I do to be as one with Jesus, to be a citizen in God's kingdom? What must I do to be whole, complete?"

"Give to the poor," Jesus says. "Give to the poor."

This Old Friend

When the disciples see Jesus praying, they ask him to teach them how to pray and he replies, pray in this way: Our Father in heaven, hallowed be your name. Your kingdom come. Your will be done, on earth as it is in heaven. Give us this day our daily bread. And forgive us our debts, as we also have forgiven our debtors. And do not bring us to the time of trial, but rescue us from the evil one. Matthew 6:9-13

I met Gerold in August. He died the next January. He had been a college professor; a bright, talkative man, his wife said. When I met him and JoLana, he did not speak a word, but simply smiled, and let me take his hand in greeting. About three years before we met he suffered a series of strokes. They gradually took away his ability to speak until he stopped talking altogether, except for an occasional yes or no.

When I came into their home for the first time, JoLana and I visited for a bit, then I asked, "Would you like to have communion?" The three of us sat at the kitchen table. I brought out two thin wafers of bread, poured wine into two small glasses, and repeated the familiar words of our Lord, "This is my body given for you. This is my blood shed for you."

Then I began to pray, "Our Father, who art in heaven ...," and I heard Gerold's voice for the first time, praying those old words with JoLana and me, each word all the way to "Amen." He received the bread and wine, I spoke a word of blessing, and Gerold went back to his chair, and said not another word.

There is this promise in Romans 8:26, "The Spirit helps us in our weakness; for we do not know how to pray as we ought, but that very Spirit intercedes with sighs too deep for words." In that moment, for Gerold, the Spirit interceded with words that were deep within him.

This was Gerald's old friend come to help him when he needed a bit of help.

We pray these words gathered around the baptismal font, as a child or adult begins her journey with Jesus. We repeat them gathered around a wood box soon to be lowered into the ground.

We say these words at worship, in Sunday School classes and Bible study groups, at the end of meetings and weddings, around the campfire at Bible Camp. At our beginning and our ending, and everywhere in between. We share them with Catholics and Methodists and Baptists and Presbyterians. Our mutual friend. For this old friend connects us to one another.

We do not pray, "My Father in heaven." We pray "Our Father" and "give us this day our daily bread." We are in this together, this thing we call faith and church and forgiveness and daily bread. If I am unable to pray because of illness or distress, you are praying on my behalf. And we are asking God to provide daily bread to all who are hungry, even as God expects us to be a part of the answer to that prayer.

This prayer is a gift from Jesus, one he taught his friends and passed on to us. I cannot help but think that he understands how we are. He made it short, so we could remember it. Simple, yet covers all the bases. And always ready to help us on the way. Like an old friend.

Come Away and Rest a While

Most every Sunday morning Stub Kaberle would come to worship, find his usual pew, and almost immediately fall asleep. Stub farmed. He worked hard all week. The church was warm and comfortable and safe. Stub was there, always faithful, giving witness to Jesus by his coming to this place of worship. He gathered with family and friends in a community of faith, getting his Sabbath, resting back in the welcome comfort of Jesus.

It was just fine. I thought it high praise that in Christ's Church, Stub Kaberle could sleep like a baby.

My last Sunday in that congregation, Stub sat up front and stayed awake the whole time. That was just fine too.

Here is a little story told in the gospel of Mark.

"The apostles gathered around Jesus and told him all that they had done and taught. He said to them, 'Come away to a deserted place all by yourselves and rest a while.' For many were coming and going, and they had no leisure even to eat. And they went away in the boat to a deserted place by themselves." Mark 6:30-32

Jesus invites his followers, you and I included, to "come away ... to a lonely place, and rest awhile." Sabbath. To rest from labor.

Through Moses, God spoke this word: "Remember the sabbath day, and keep it holy." Sabbath. Many tie it to worship because Martin Luther took that commandment and wrote this meaning: "We are to fear and love God, so that we do not despise the preaching of God's word, but instead keep that word holy and gladly hear and learn it."

Luther is telling us that keeping the third commandment means setting aside time to worship, to go to church, which is fine. But there is another truth about this word to "remember the Sabbath day and keep it holy."

My Old Testament professor at Luther Seminary, John Milton, said the Commandments were given to Israel, not to make them God's people, but because they already were God's people. The Ten Commandments were given to a nation recently set free from slavery in Egypt. God was reminding the people of the words recorded in Genesis, that after "... God finished the work that God had done, God rested on the seventh day from all the work that God had done." God rested from labor. Just so God set aside a time for rest for God's people.

For Israel this word did not feel like a rule or a law or a commandment. It felt like grace. It was a word spoken to a people who were slaves, who did not work a 40-hour week, get most weekends off and have four weeks of vacation each year. They were slaves. Now they were free, and God was telling them to take a sabbath, to rest awhile.

A friend retired. After a few weeks he came to me and said, "I feel guilty. I feel as if I am not worth as much anymore." His work gave him worth. A reason to be. And so it is that one of the first things we ask people when we meet is "What do you do?" Or, "Where do you work?"

One of my teachers, Gerhard Frost, wrote, "I'm breaking my habit of asking strangers 'What do you do?' as if they're no more than what they do."

I don't know if I have ever met the person who said, as he or she looked back upon their life, "I wish I would have worked more."

Do we not rather say, "I wish I would have spent more time with my children. I wish I would have told him how much he meant to me.

I wish I would have listened to the stories my parents told. I wish I would have laughed more, loved more, helped more, thanked more."

The one who invites us to "come away" and "rest awhile" is also the one who invites us who are weary and heavy laden to come to him, for he says, "I will give you rest." Jesus is our Sabbath. Jesus is our rest. In the faith that he is present, in the faith that he forgives, in the faith that God is ever near, in the faith that we are loved, there is rest. Stop trying so hard. Let God love you.

Dear child, God does not say today, "Be strong."
He knows your strength is spent. He knows how long
The road has been, how weary you have grown.
For He who walked the earthly roads along
Each boggy lowland and each rugged hill,
Can understand, and so he says, "Be still,
And know that I AM GOD." The hour is late
And you must rest awhile, and you must wait
Until life's empty reservoirs fill up,
As slow rains fill an empty upturned cup.
Hold up your cup, dear child, for God to fill:
He only asks today that you be still.

— "For the One Who Is Tired," by Grace Noll Crowell (1877-1969)

"The time you enjoy wasting is not wasted time."
— Bertrand Russell (1872-1970)

So take a load off. Sit a spell. Take a nap. Get some sleep. Take it easy. Come away and rest awhile.

I Saw Good Friday

on the news last night.
I witnessed the hate
and fear,
heard the shouts
of rage,
saw the contorted faces
of anger.
A tall blonde woman,
perhaps beautiful
in repose,
raised her arms,
folded her fingers
into a fist
and shook
until her beauty
left.
There must have been
fathers and mothers
there to meet
the buses carrying
the children.
They yelled
and swore,
waved their signs
until the buses left.
I saw Good Friday
on the news last night,
heard the descendants
of immigrants
shout crucify.
Crucify.

Hope at the Hardware Store

It is spring.
I need help with my lawn.
It is full of dandelions and quack grass.
I go to the hardware store,
where the wood floor sounds like yesterday.
There I will find
(along with nuts, bolts, screwdrivers, and lawnmowers)
fertilizer and weed killer.
She stands behind the counter,
with her black hair and gentle smile.
I ask, *do you know anything?*
Yes, she says.
I need help, I say.
I tell her about my yard.
I tell her how I failed in the fall to feed the lawn.
She gently shakes her head,
smiles this gentle smile,
which is both a confirmation of my neglect
(my sin really)
and an absolution.
The smile says you are forgiven.
She says, *you can begin again, it will be alright.*
I borrow a spreader for a couple of hours.
I go home and begin once again.
I bring the spreader back.
Jim is there behind the counter.
I ask about the woman
with the black hair and the gentle smile.
I tell my story.
She gave me hope, I say.

That would be Paula, he says.
She is just that way.
A blessing then upon Paula.
A blessing upon all those who give us hope,
whose lives are just that way.
In a world full of discouraging words,
what a grace it is to hear a word of hope.
It's like bumping into Jesus.

Four Girls Baking Hope

i went to the bread part of the store
looking for a loaf of bread
of course
i heard them first
then looked up to see
all four dressed in white
from top to toe
going about the business
of getting bread ready
for folks like me
working
and talking
and laughing
all at the same time
enjoying
each other's company
it made me smile
and
gave me hope
for the world

Rain

He farms.
So depends on the weather
more than most.
Rain, he said.
Rain.
It's free.
Remarkable.
So valuable.
Yet it is free.
It does not cost me anything.
But you cannot buy it
at any price.

Delight

Here are some words about wisdom found in the book of Proverbs, chapter 8.

The Lord created me at the beginning of his work,
the first of his acts of long ago.
Ages ago I was set up,
at the first, before the beginning of the earth.
When he established the heavens, I was there,
when he marked out the foundations of the earth,
then I was beside him, like a master worker;
and I was daily his delight,
rejoicing before him always,
rejoicing in his inhabited world
and delighting in the human race.

My mother attended school through eighth grade. Then she was needed at home. I remember how she delighted in her children. But as I think back, I realize that she delighted in everyone she met. She delighted in humanity. Educated? No. Wise? Never a doubt.

Wisdom is not learned from books. Wisdom is from God. This poem from Proverbs has wisdom proclaiming that she was, "The beginning of God's work, the first of God's acts of long ago," even bragging, "I was daily God's delight."

It would seem then that wisdom is not the accumulation of facts nor the recitation of those facts. Wisdom has an agenda. Wisdom rejoices in God's inhabited world and delights in the human race. Watch a grandmother holding her grandchild. You will see delight.

The book of James encourages us to pray for wisdom. I would suggest that James is encouraging us to pray for delight. Pray that we might not just delight in our own, but in humanity. Delight in everyone we meet along the way.

Entrusted

We are told in the first chapter of Genesis that God created both male and female in God's image and then told them to, "Be fruitful and multiply, and fill the earth and subdue it."

Psalm 8 prays, "When I look at your heavens, the work of your fingers, the moon and the stars that you have established; what are human beings that you are mindful of them, mortals that you care for them? Yet you have made them a little lower than God, and crowned them with glory and honor. You have given them dominion over the works of your hands; you have put all things under their feet, all sheep and oxen, and also the beasts of the field, the birds of the air, and the fish of the sea, whatever passes along the paths of the seas."

"A little lower than God, and crowned with glory and honor …." That's us, folks. You and me. "… given dominion over the works of your (God's) hands." Well we sure have screwed that up.

We drive out to a remote spot in the country to watch the sunrise. We marvel at the greatness of God, give thanks for the beauty of this place. Then as we drive off, we throw our trash out the window.

I lived in a lake community. A friend who had lived most of his life in that place, told me that when he was much younger, he could see the bottom of the lake. No more.

We have been entrusted. And we have failed.

Repentance is not simply mouthing practiced words. Repentance means to turn around, to go in a different direction, a new way. Mom goes into her child's room and finds a huge mess. The son says, "Sorry Mom." Mom says, "Sorry doesn't cut it. Clean up your room."

Trust

The Apostle Paul is remarkable in his faith. In his letter to the congregation in Rome, he writes about his suffering and comes to this conclusion: "we also boast in our sufferings, knowing that suffering produces endurance, and endurance produces character, and character produces hope, and hope does not disappoint us, because God's love has been poured into our hearts through the Holy Spirit that has been given to us." Romans 5

I had knee surgery, which was not a lot of fun, but the knee got better and the pain went away. So no suffering. I've never been in prison, never faced the possibility of being put to death for my faith. So I have some difficulty relating to Paul.

I think suffering produces anger, which produces self-pity, which produces hopelessness. Paul thinks otherwise. No poor me. Rather trust. Easy to trust when things are going well, but Paul wants to teach us to trust, to have faith even when everything is not coming up roses. Paul is saying even when it seems otherwise, God is still present. Trust.

When I get up in the middle of the night, I can't always see my bed when I come creeping back. But it is there. And when I fall back onto it, it still holds me. Trust.

The Spirit of Truth

One of my teachers at Luther Seminary said something like this about the doctrine of the Trinity. It is a teaching we cannot explain; it is a teaching we cannot deny.

And so we confess, I believe in God the Father ... I believe in God the Son ... I believe in God the Spirit ... one in three and three in one.

Another professor said it is not the task of the Church to lift up, or even understand the Holy Spirit, rather it is the Spirit's task to reveal Jesus, and if Jesus is being followed, then the Spirit is doing her work. Jesus agrees, for he says, "The Spirit will glorify me ... will take what is mine and declare it ...."

When Jesus is brought before Pilate, Jesus says, "For this I was born ... to testify to the truth." (John 18:37) Pilate asks, "What is truth?" Jesus doesn't answer. The question just hangs there. Pilate, looking truth in the eye, still could not see. Perhaps it was the wrong question. Not what, rather who?

It is not right doctrine that saves, not belonging to the right denomination that is the truth. We will differ as Christians on a whole bunch of stuff, but none of that stuff is finally the truth.

Jesus sets us free to disagree with each other and free to hold a variety of opinions on a variety of subjects. Our oneness, our hope, our salvation, our faith, is in him. So we rest back, all of us, in the love of God, knowing we need not find cause to justify ourselves, for we are justified already by the grace of God through faith in Jesus, who is our truth.

Mystery. Our calling, our work is not to solve the mystery. Jesus does not invite us to explain God. Jesus calls us to follow him, to be his love in this world.

Don't worry too much about the rest.

The following two poems were written for the 500th anniversary of the Reformation, and read at a celebration held on Wednesday, November 1, 2017, at the Sioux Falls Arena in Sioux Falls, South Dakota.

<u>1517</u>

fear
fear of hell
fear of damnation
fear of separation
fear of lightening in the sky
"St. Anne, help me, I will become a monk."
because it is not just lightning in the sky
listen
listen
my church
my people
hear the word
to Zechariah
and to Mary
to the shepherds in the night
"Do not be afraid."
do not be afraid
and yet
and yet the Church
is filled with fear
God's children afraid
afraid of God
the wrath of God
and where are the pastors
speaking comfort
"As soon as the coin in the coffer rings,
a soul from purgatory springs."
selling passports to heaven
preaching fear

preaching separation
preaching damnation
unless you open your purse
do not be afraid, said the angel to the shepherds
do not fear, Jesus said to the disciples
yet fear in the church
because of the shape of the church
reshape
reform
renew
question
always question
reformation
re for mation
to form again
to change
to shape again
go back to the beginning
for in the beginning was the word
and the word was with God
and the word was God
and the word became flesh
and lived among us
back to that beginning
back to that word
that became flesh
and lived among us
this is my son
listen to him
do not be afraid, he says
have no fear little flock, he says
I go to prepare a place for you
so that where I am there you
will be also
read it for yourselves

now dear believers
read the scriptures for yourselves
now my children
read of God's love and mercy
you priests of God
you bishops of God
read the word of God
in your own language
for the true treasure of the Church
is the Holy Gospel
and do not be afraid
for what God asks is your faith
not your purse
baptism is the only indulgence
necessary for salvation
all of life is a return
to baptism
cling to your baptism
my children
cling to the promises of God
cling to God's grace
my church
make your entire life to be one of repentance
and trust in Christ alone
and so become Christ to your neighbor
on a Wednesday in October
in 1517
a 33-year-old pastor
son to Hans and Margaret
dared to question
dared to say enough
no more
and so it began

2017

so much has changed
we live in a very different world
we don't see the devil behind
every rock and tree
our streets are clean
our children educated
most people live long lives
Bibles are all over the place
waiting to be opened
we trust that even in death
we are safe in God's care
and yet
and yet
what do we fear today
and we do fear today
but not damnation
not hell
certainly not the clergy
but still
but still
there is fear
not fear of God
not fear of God's wrath
mostly we fear one another
but especially
we fear those people
you know those people
different people
different color
different language
different faith
names we cannot pronounce
they don't look like us

they don't worship like us
they don't talk like us
why can't they learn to talk like us
what are they doing here anyway
I invite you listen to William Shakespeare
as he speaks through Shylock
in Merchant of Venice
"I am a Jew. Hath not a Jew eyes? Hath not a Jew hands, organs, dimensions, senses, affections, passions? Fed with the same food, hurt with the same weapons, subject to the same diseases, healed by the same means, warmed and cooled by the same winter and summer as a Christian is? If you prick us, do we not bleed? If you tickle us, do we not laugh? If you poison us, do we not die?"
Shylock speaks not only as a Jew in his time, but he speaks in our
time for
the poor
the female
the Muslim
the transgender
the gay and lesbian
the immigrant
the undocumented
the indigenous people
anyone who is looked upon as being less
1517
2017
so much has changed
so much is different
yet so much is the same
"If you prick us, do we not bleed? If you tickle us, do we not laugh? If you poison us, do we not die?"
and so as Luther did

we go
back to the beginning
for in the beginning
was the word
and the word was with God
and the word was God
and the word became flesh
and lived among us
and the one who said
to the church in 1517
do not be afraid
have no fear little flock
I am with you always
says to the church in 2017
did you not see what I did
did you not notice
how I went about
when I stopped by the town well
and visited with a woman
I treated her as an equal
it is 2017 and you still have
not figured out that
such has been my intent
since the beginning
when I created both
male and female in my image
and did you not make note
of the fact that I spent
much time eating with
people who were considered less
2017
many say the church is irrelevant

maybe they are right
each Sunday we come
into the building
confess our sins
hear absolution
sing our hymns
pray our prayers
we know how to be in church
in 2017 can the church be the church
maybe it is a matter of memory
we forget who we are
we forget
that God created humankind
all of humankind
in God's image
after God's likeness
and when we forget
we get scared
and we build walls
remember who you are
you are a child of God
marked with the cross of Christ forever
and so we always go back
to the beginning
as Luther did
back to the one
who said
have no fear, little flock
for he is the one who
treated women as equals
the one who ate with
those considered less

we need not move to a new place
rather we go back again and again
to that one who bids us come follow
then sends us out
to be little Christs in this world
are we free enough to not be safe
do we have courage enough to go back to faith
it has been said that faith
can move mountains

what mountains need moving

Two Easters

There are perhaps two Easters.
The one waiting for us
when our time on this earth has ended,
that morning surprise
when we are raised up from death to life,
gathered to our parents,
put back on our feet again
in that place that Jesus went ahead
and prepared for us,
where every tear is wiped away
and death is no more.

But there is this Easter now,
when we rise up
to meet the day,
hearing a benediction upon our lives,
maybe a little loose in the joints,
a bit shabby and worn,
perhaps misunderstood by others,
but knowing that in this world
often enamored with that which is a lie,
a fake,
we have discovered that which is truth,
which is real;
we have discovered the grand secret
of the Kingdom of God.

Not Just Another Pretty Face

the great faces
the ones we recognize immediately
the ones that grace covers of magazines
that we carry in our billfolds in case
they don't take a credit card
the ones that get carved in mountains
or whose likeness hangs on a museum wall
and are remembered
generation after generation
those faces are not necessarily
beautiful or handsome
they would not be spotted by some agent who
says you should be in the movies
I can get you a contract
no the great faces
weren't born to it
they earned their way
they worked
they struggled
they fought
they learned from their mistakes
they did not give up
they achieved
and the most important part
of a great face
is not the eyes
think of Helen Keller
or the ears
remember Lincoln
and not even the mouth

consider Washington
with his wooden teeth
rather what makes
a great face
is what lies behind
the eyes
what is between
the ears
what comes out of
the mouth
that's what makes
a memorable face
not a beautiful face
or a handsome face
not even a pretty face
but a great face

My Good Friend, Afraid and Brave at the Same Time

My good friend — a kind and gentle woman of faith and compassion, with a great sense of humor — was diagnosed with ALS.

Some say that faith in God will fix life. Believe in Jesus and all will be well. Put your trust in God and God will deliver security and even wealth.

By the late 1930s, Adolf Hitler had taken control of the Christian Church in Germany. Many leaders in the Church were silent. But one young pastor named Dietrich Bonhoeffer, a pacifist, joined a conspiracy to "rid the world of a madman." In a Christmas greeting in 1940, Bonhoeffer wrote that in the Church, "Germans ... want a 'vacation from life,' 'a wisp of magic asking nothing and promising everything.'" (*Strange Glory* by Charles Marsh, p. 302) Bonhoeffer was imprisoned and hanged just before the war ended.

The Apostle Paul, in prison awaiting trial, wrote a letter to a congregation in the city of Philippi, which includes these words: "... for I have learned to be content with whatever I have." (Philippians 4:11) It is a remarkable testimony of faith in the worst of times, but faith did not get Paul out of jail. He remained in prison until he was executed.

In many Christian Churches, the Sunday before Lent is called Transfiguration Sunday and the gospel reading is the story of Jesus and three members of his congregation walking to the top of a mountain, where Jesus' appearance is changed (transfigured); "his face shone like the sun, and his clothes became dazzling white." The disciples hear a voice declaring, "This is my son, the beloved; with him I am well pleased ...." (Matthew 17)

That beloved son is eventually betrayed, beaten, and nailed to a cross, where he is heard to cry with a loud voice, "My God, my God, why have you forsaken me?" (Matthew 27)

We live on this side of Easter, so we believe Jesus was not forsaken, but was raised up from death to life, that he lives. But at the time of his great suffering, he, too, asked "why." Why is this happening to me? What have I done to deserve this? Why is God allowing this to happen? Has God abandoned me?

There is good evidence that two of the disciples with Jesus on that mountain died for their faith in him. Faith in God did not guarantee comfort or wealth, or freedom from troubles.

The blessings that flow from faith may have a greater impact upon the neighbor than upon the one who is faithful.

I am not sure if I know how to say this, but I believe that my friend's faith, her grace and compassion, her kindness and gentleness, were no guarantee she would be saved from troubles, but it did guarantee she would be a blessing to others. Her faith in Jesus was not a promise that her troubles would be over and her life full of joy. But her faith in Jesus was a promise that she would strive to help others in their troubles, and she would bring joy to this world. She made a difference.

I do not understand why this world is filled with so much injustice and suffering. Some has been caused by our own greed and selfishness. We are sinners and therefore we sin. We do wrong to one another in many ways. We bring hurt to those we love and even to ourselves.

So perhaps we can explain, even though it seems impossible to comprehend, the imprisonment and execution of people like Paul and Bonhoeffer. We only get to chapter four in Genesis before Cain kills his own brother. Much of the pain and suffering we witness is on us.

But that does not answer all our questions. How can God, who we confess to be all good and, at the same time, all powerful, allow illness and calamity to come down upon God's children? How could God allow my good friend to suffer a lifetime of broken bones and pain.

It does not take long on this earth to discover that some things do not make any sense, no matter how we may try to explain them.

Maybe there is a plan, as some say. In truth, I do not know. I am pretty sure no one else on this earth knows either. But it is hard to see God's purpose when you are diagnosed with ALS or cancer, or when you lose a child, or when a flood comes raging through your community, or when you have a heart attack at age 50, or your spouse begins to show signs of dementia.

When those things happen, somehow you still believe. You still pray. You still strive, as best you can, to follow Jesus and do what you can to help others in their need, but there are times, many times when you want to raise your voice loudly and cry, "My God, my God, why?"

Jesus said to them, "Truly I tell you, the tax collectors and the prostitutes are going into the kingdom of God ahead of you."
Matthew 21:31

It Was Not Our Sin

it was not our sin
that crucified Jesus
not our sin
that placed that crown of thorns
upon his head
that whipped his back until he bled
it was not our sin
Jesus went about forgiving sin
from the very beginning
God forgave sin
God got used to it
got good at it
we go in the wrong direction
God says turn around
we miss the mark
God says try again
we build a barrier between
God reaches across
Jesus is his name and
sinners welcomed him
ate with him
were comfortable with him
for sure he rubbed some people
the wrong way
but not the sinners
they liked him

they liked him a lot
what's not to like
good storyteller
makes water into wine
great with kids
doesn't yell
maybe once but not usually
no it was not our sin
that nailed him to that tree
it was our righteousness
that killed Jesus
our need to be right
our continuous day after day
effort to always be right
about everything and
everyone
our need to build walls
between
to keep the sinners out
this desire to be god
to create a world that
suits us
a world full of people
created in our image
after our likeness
so Jesus could not live
for he wills to set us free
from ourselves
set us free to serve
one another
set us free to be
who we are
a people imperfect

and broken
yet in love with God
in love with humanity
in love with the earth
for God is at work in us
and
Jesus came to live
that truth
but we will not have it

Fear

someone tells you
to not be afraid
as if by telling you
to not be afraid
all of a sudden
you will not be afraid
never worked with me
we are told in the Bible that
God tells us
to not be afraid
and it is a good thing to hear
but there are times
i am still afraid

Sitting in My Favorite Chair, Covered by My Favorite Blanket

Once upon a time a good doctor opened my right leg, took out the knee I was born with and put in another. I had been told that total knee replacement surgery is hard. But I found that not to be true. I went to sleep one Monday morning and woke up a short time later with a new knee. No problem. Knee surgery is easy. I slept through it.

Learning to use the new knee was another matter. I discovered that I am a wimp. I am very good at sitting in my favorite chair, covered by my favorite blanket, being waited upon by my most favorite nurse, who also happens to be my favorite wife. But physical therapy is not my strong suit.

Still, it continued, as it should, despite my protests, because of the encouragement of caregivers who came into our home and pushed me, and then pushed me some more.

In the gospel of John, chapter 14, verse 12, we read these words spoken by Jesus to his disciples, to the Church: "Very truly, I tell you, the one who believes in me will also do the works that I do and, in fact, will do greater works than these, because I am going to the Father."

I am not confident that I understand all that Jesus is saying, but I will argue that he is promising that his good work of healing continues every day, all over the world. It continues through the minds and skilled hands of doctors, nurses, therapists, teachers, counselors, farmers, storekeepers and ordinary neighbors. During that time of sitting in my favorite chair, my good neighbor steered his lawn mower onto our property. I believe he was doing the work of Jesus.

Anytime healing comes, anytime good happens, Jesus is at work.

Many years ago, one of my wise teachers said, "We thank God for all that is good. We do not blame God for the bad." That is a good way to live, a good faith to hold on to. I do not need to sort out all that is happening each day, but I simply trust that God intends good and not evil, and when evil does come, it is not God punishing, but rather gives testimony to the reality that we live in a broken world, where bad things do happen to good people.

But that is not God's intention. God's plan is for good. There is a verse in the Old Testament, words from the mouth of the prophet Jeremiah: "I know the plans I have for you, says the Lord, plans for your welfare and not for harm, to give you a future with hope." (Jeremiah 29:11)

We thank God for all that is good. We do not blame God for the bad. When one is in the midst of troubles, it is difficult to hold on to such faith. When the therapist told me to push that knee back, push it back some more, I was not capable of seeing the good she intended. I only knew that moment of pain. But she did intend good for me and was asking me to trust.

Jesus is at work all over the place, every day, doing good, bringing healing. One of our tasks as the Church is to recognize that truth, to point it out, and to give thanks to God. I might also suggest that you and I give thanks to that doctor or teacher or spouse or neighbor who is doing the work of Jesus.

Driving in St. Paul

Recently Vivian and I went back to St. Paul and Luther Seminary for a class reunion. Our drive went well, but it is not rural South Dakota. Leaving the city behind, I was attempting to find the turn I needed to get us out of town. I was not keeping up. And to let me know I was not keeping up, a gentleman (I assume a male, since this seemed like the way a male would respond to such a situation) started honking his horn.

I began to wonder why. Out loud, I began to wonder why. What good are you doing? Your honking will not cause me to drive faster, because I have good reason to drive at this speed. I do not know this road or the turn I am looking for, so it behooves me to drive at a speed that will give me the greatest opportunity of finding what I need to find at this time in my life.

He honked again anyway. And I continued to drive at my desired speed. And he continued to honk. I guess one could say that we agreed to disagree.

It Does Not Take Much

I went for a walk this morning. I found a dime. Pretty roughed up. Been there for a while. There was a time when a dime would get you an ice cream cone or a bag of popcorn, let you park downtown at a meter for a few minutes. Not anymore.

But that morning that dime brought me joy. I even told my wife later, "I found a dime today." I put it on my desk and there it now sits, my dime, which I found.

I plan to keep it. On my desk. I want to see it once in a while, to remind me of a small blessing that came without planning or promise. It just showed up. Like most blessings do. Unexpected, unplanned, undeserved. Bringing joy. It does not take much.

Most every day, Vivian and I go for a walk, and when weather permits, we usually walk one of the bike paths near Lewis and Clark Lake.

One day we came upon a Frisbee disc on the path. I said, "Someone must have lost this." So I picked it up and then saw another just a few feet ahead. "Well that's strange, two discs." It was then that we both looked up and saw six young adults, several yards ahead of us. One of them was waving his golf disc in our direction. I quickly put the disc down where I had found it. Then I prepared my apology as we walked toward the group.

I tell you this story not so much to brag about my intelligence or my ability to disrupt a game of disc golf, but to share with you the kindness of strangers. "No problem," they laughed, "we were just playing for fun." And off they went with smiles and off we went laughing at ourselves and better for having met these kind folk. It may seem like a small thing, but that day they blessed us with gentle laughter and kindness.

I have told this story before, but I like it, so will share again. Lucas was our neighbor for a while when we lived in Watertown. He was of an age when it is okay for a boy to cry, especially when he falls and scrapes his knee, which is what he did one day. I happened to be outside and so I heard his cry. I walked over to see if I could help, as did his two older brothers.

We all asked, in unison, "Are you okay? Did you hurt your knee?" We could plainly see that he had, but we asked anyway. His mom came out, picked him up, hugged him, looked at his knee, and asked if he wanted a Band Aid. He was still crying when I asked, "Would you like a licorice?" At the word "licorice" he stopped crying. Immediately. He looked at me and nodded "yes." Ah, I thought, the healing power of licorice.

I am not recommending licorice in place of Mom's holding and hugging, nor in place of a Band Aid. But licorice can help. When I asked Lucas if he wanted a licorice, I was saying, I care about you. Sometimes licorice is enough.

Years ago, Vivian and I were in Silver Spring, Maryland, babysitting our two grandsons. The boys were still in school and each day the four of us walked the half mile to and back together. One morning it looked like it might rain, so I suggested we drive. Finn, who was seven, said, "No, let's walk. I like to walk and talk."

When he is "walking and talking" with his grandma or grandpa for that half-mile, he has our full attention. No television blaring in the background, no newspaper in front of my nose, no video game tempting him to "come, play." Just two people sharing lives.

It is how Jesus spent his life. It is what still attracts me to him.

The stories of his raising the dead or walking on water or changing water into wine only confuse me because they seem so far away from what I have experienced in life.

But those little scenes, those brief encounters with ordinary people still encourage and invite me.

He took time to sit down at the village well and have conversation with a woman of a different faith and not the best reputation. He invites himself to the home of a guy he sees up a tree, a guy who is working for Rome collecting taxes. He invites a child to share his lunch with a whole bunch of adults.

May not seem like much, but each one of these people would have been considered less and Jesus treated each one with respect and dignity. He was always leaning towards inclusiveness. He was always opening his arms in welcome to those the religious folk wanted to keep out. He noticed people and he paid attention to people. He was doing something that all of us can do.

Ordinary, common, everyday compassion.

So maybe a morning question is this: How can I make this day just a little better for someone? It matters not family, friend, or stranger. For each is a child that God loves.

It does not take much.

Identity

We are in our living room. I am sitting in a chair. Vivian is on the floor, playing with grandson Finn, who is four years old. Brother Benjamin, six years old, is also on the floor with a truck. Benjamin soon discovers that if he pushes down on the truck while moving it in a circle, the truck will squeak. Benjamin goes around and around in a circle, near Finn, and all the while the truck is going squeak, squeak, squeak. It is truly an irritating, obnoxious sound. This goes on for some time and I notice that Benjamin has a slight smile on his face. Finally, Finn jumps up, raises his arms in the air, and shouts, "He's driving me crazy." Then he picks up a plastic toy and throws it at his brother, aiming, I am pretty sure, for his head. The boys give evidence of original sin. They are sinners, and we eat with them. But we see them with different eyes. They are our grandsons first. That is what defines them; that is their identity. When Jesus walked this earth, the religious leaders usually saw people as either good or bad. Jesus saw with different eyes. He saw them as God's children, and he ate with them.

Here is Faith

A preschool teacher told this story. She said that the children are supposed to be three years old and potty trained, but sometimes ....

One day, a little boy had an accident. The teacher had to change him. As she was doing so, he looked up at her, smiled a big smile, and said, "Don't you just love me?"

If we could have such faith in God.

Who Is This Guy?

Traveling from Washington to South Dakota, Vivian and I took a route through North Dakota. We stopped near Medora. Looking around a visitor's center, a man came up and said, "Hi Gary, what are you doing here?" Who was this guy? No idea. He must have noticed my bewilderment because he said, "Jim. Your cousin." Of course it was. But I did not recognize him because he should not have been there. He lives in Rugby, not Medora. We live in South Dakota. What are the odds? Same place, same day, same time? He should not have been there.

There is a story in the gospel of Luke (chapter 24) about two disciples of Jesus who are walking together from Jerusalem to the village of Emmaus. It's about a seven-mile walk. As they walk along this other guy shows up and walks with them. They don't have a clue who this guy is, but he seems harmless, so they walk together and tell this stranger about Jesus and that they are sad.

The guy, of course, is Jesus, but they don't recognize him. For those disciples, it's all past tense. "He was a prophet." "We had hoped." Of course they did not recognize him. He should not have been there.

Neither one of them should have been there. Jim or Jesus.

But Jim was there in Medora. And Jesus was there on the road. Jim spoke, took my hand in greeting, looked me in the eye and I recognized him and was glad to see him again.

When those two disciples stopped for supper, they asked this guy to join them. He did. And during the meal, he broke bread, and these two old friends recognized him. In the breaking of the bread.

We still do.

Remembering Ed Sullivan and Other Dusty People

I was driving alone one day and suddenly, for no reason, Ed Sullivan popped into my head. I have no idea, but I said out loud, "Ed Sullivan." Now some of you reading this may have no idea of who I am talking about. Ed Sullivan was on television every Sunday night for 23 years. From the time I was 8 years old until I was 31, Ed Sullivan hosted a one-hour variety show. He introduced America to The Beatles. Most of America turned on their televisions Sunday evening to watch the Ed Sullivan Show.

And yet today there are perhaps three generations who have no idea of who I am writing about, unless they watch Stephen Colbert and hear that the show is being broadcast from the Ed Sullivan Theatre in New York City.

In the Christian Church there is a time of preparation for Easter called Lent. The beginning of Lent is Ash Wednesday. One of rituals of Ash Wednesday is the marking of ashes on the forehead and hearing the words, "Remember that you are dust, and to dust you shall return."

It is a reminder of our mortality, that our life upon this earth is brief. And truth be told, even the memory of our time upon this earth is brief. Most of us are forgotten within a generation.

We are dust.

But it is amazing what God can do with dust. We are told in Genesis (chapter 2) that God formed humankind from the dust of the ground and breathed into that dust the breath of life. And if God can do such with dust, He can do other marvelous things.

The fact is we are a dusty people, prone to selfishness and violence. Our faith is that God still loves us and has high expectations of us.

The fact is all of us will finally be put in the ground and returned to dust. Our faith is that God will raise us from that ground, from dust, and breathe life into that dust again.

The fact is most of us will not be long remembered. Our faith is that God does indeed remember us in life and in death.

The fact is our time upon this earth is brief, fleeting. We have only now, this day. Our faith is "this is the day that the Lord has made, let us rejoice and be glad in it."

God desires us to live this day thankful for the gift that it is, and in such a way that it will be a better day for another who shares this day with us.

The fact is we are dust. Our faith is that God can do wonderful things with dust.

August 29, 2006

Today, in South Dakota,
we plan to kill a man,
the state, all of us, so
students in school
have the opportunity
for discussion, and over
lunch, between bites,
old men can debate
gas prices and lethal
injection, and a woman
questioned at the mall
says she wants to
be there to watch, but
a high school student
has homecoming
to plan, so hasn't
thought much about
this man who will die,
who did a terrible
thing, who killed
another human being,
and today we plan to show
this man how wrong
it is to kill another
human being, by
killing a human
being. Today, in
South Dakota the
shepherd will leave
the ninety-nine in the
wilderness, go off
after the one which
is lost, and when he
has found it, he will
lay it on his shoulder
and cut its throat.

A Family Member

Vivian and I were on a bus trip returning home. We got off the bus for a few minutes. On the way back to the bus, I saw this young woman pulling full garbage bags out of containers, putting in empty bags. Her route covers 90 miles on the interstate. She drives her own truck, buys her own gas and is paid $9 per hour. She seemed tired, defeated. And I cannot seem to forget her.

Lord, when was it we saw you?

... And To Dust You Shall Return

Here is one of my favorite poems, by Jane Kenyon, entitled "Otherwise."

*I got out of bed
on two strong legs.
It might have been
otherwise. I ate
cereal, sweet
milk, ripe, flawless
peach. It might
have been otherwise.
I took the dog uphill
to the birch wood.
All morning I did
the work I love.
At noon I lay down
with my mate. It might
have been otherwise.
We ate dinner together
at a table with silver
candlesticks. It might
have been otherwise.
I slept in a bed
in a room with paintings
on the walls, and
planned another day
just like this day.
But one day, I know
it will be otherwise.*

Jane Kenyon died in April of 1995. She was 48 years old.

"Remember that you are dust and to dust you shall return." The familiar words of Ash Wednesday, a reminder of our mortality.

I was visiting with a funeral director. He said they were keeping a body for a much later burial. He told of the work involved, how difficult it is to keep a body because "the body wants to return to the earth."

I have two knees. My right knee is no longer original. The left one gets a tight wrap put around it every morning. The good doctor who replaced my right knee said that eventually I will need to do the same with my left knee. What this does, of course, is to remind me, in yet another way, of my mortality.

When I think of my own dying it is not so much with a sense of fear as with a feeling of great sadness. I have grown accustomed to this place, this world. I like living on this earth. My knees remind me it is temporary.

Remembering that we are dust is a sobering but good thing. Our days are limited, therefore we count the blessings of each one. Every day is a gift.

The 40 days of Lent come out of the 40 days that Jesus spent in the wilderness, alone, hungry, questioning his identity. The tempter raises the question, "If you are the Son of God …." Inferring otherwise. It was hard, but Jesus discovered, in that wilderness, that he was not alone, that his life had purpose, that he was God's child.

Where can one find wilderness these days? A place where we discover what is important, what is essential and good, and a place where we find out who we really are.

A friend will call for help, someone you love needs your attention, your child is in trouble, your health changes. These are all wilderness places where you don't want to go, places you didn't ask for, but you are led there anyway, and there you discover who you really are. You find that you are not alone, for God is there too, and you are braver and wiser and have more faith than you ever imagined.

That wilderness place is also a place of grace. For there you learn that God will use you to do his work in this world and you will be a blessing. You help the friend who calls. You use whatever wealth you might have to do good. You pay attention to the ones you love.

May this season of Lent be for you a kind of wilderness place, where you discover once again who you are, a child of God, with a purpose in God's world.

Don't let the mistakes you made, the wrongs you did yesterday, dictate what you do today. Something happens when you confess your sin. You are forgiven.

If we keep looking back, we are hampered in our work. Remember the old joke about the guy who comes to his doctor, holds up his hand, waves it about, and says, "It hurts when I do that." The doctor says, "Well, then don't do that."

Jesus says, "Don't keep looking back at who you were. Today, you are my disciple, and there is good work to do."

There was a long and hard rain, the town in the valley was under water. The citizens all gathered on a hillside. Someone pointed, said, "Look at that. There is hat going back and forth, back and forth in the water. What in the world is that?" Someone asked, "What day is it? Tuesday. Okay, then, that's George down there, because he said that he was going to mow his lawn on Tuesday, come hell or high water."

Come hell or high water, there is work to do. There are neighbors all around, some next door, some down the road, some far away, some you will never meet, but you are needed. There is good work to be done. What you do with your life matters.

I have a CD by the Nitty Gritty Dirt Band on which there is this little exchange before a song. John Denver is getting ready to sing and play, and he says to the band members, "Is this practice?" One of the band members replies, "They're all practice."

That kind of describes life. It's all practice. There is no perfection in us, and there need not be, for in Jesus we are all perfected, so we can practice with faith and with joy, doing good in this world.

A man — not a young man, either — was exercising. He was asked what he thought he was doing. He said, "I plan to live forever," then paused and said, "so far, so good."

We are indeed God's dusty people, but maybe you're not ready for the ground just yet. You have some life left to live, some God work yet to do. So far, so good.

Pastor

it is more than a title
it is an identity
not just what one does
it is who one is
a pastor
a shepherd
one who leads to pasture
the root word means
to tend
to keep
to guard
to protect
may get a call at 3 in the morning
may have a funeral on one's day off
may have a wedding rehearsal
that brings thoughts of homicide
upon the mother of the bride
will sit with those
who find themselves
in a place they thought they
would never be
will tend to the sick
keep watch over the lonely
guard the defenseless
protect the children
servant
teacher
so we will hear you say
how can I help you
what do you need
can I pray for you

you will say
let me tell you a story
let me tell you about God's love
let me tell you about Jesus
now you tell me about you
it will not always be easy.
but what a joy
what a privilege
to be a pastor
who else gets to enter the
hospital room of a new mother
gets to hold her just born child
who else gets to stand
shoulder to shoulder with family
as they lay a loved one in the earth
who else gets to spend
a life telling people good news
because she's a pastor.
this one-time stranger
who came from another place
and became our pastor
our shepherd
who led us to pasture,
set us to grazing
fed us stories of Jesus
washed us with water and word
put bread and wine and
God in our mouths

The Church is a Quilt

a multi-layered textile
a patchwork
created from individual
pieces of cloth
each piece lovingly stitched
to the other
to form
three layers of fabric
a trinity
yet one quilt
a whole
coming out of many
bringing physical comfort
while holding
love and memories
made from cloth
that already have a history
each piece of fabric
unique
each different from the other
yet each indispensable
each with
its own history
its own flaws
its own beauty
sewn together
stitched together
woven together
into one
to offer
warmth

and shelter
and comfort
or gift
marking life events
birth
graduation
marriage
leaving
coming home
all the while
holding memories
of the creator
the quilter
one coming out of many
the church is a quilt
telling stories of the quilter
and Jesus is the quilter

Some Thoughts About the Sacraments

You know how it is when you like someone and you want to show that person that you like him or her, and you tell that person, "I like you," but you want to do something special to show that person how much you like them. What do you do? You buy that person a present. Maybe a box of candy or flowers or something else that you know this person really likes.

God does the same thing. God says with words in the Bible, "I love you." Then God says, "I want to tell you that I love you with two very special gifts." We call those gifts sacraments.

God said to you even before you knew anything about God, "I love you." Then God gave you a gift to show you that love. Your mom and dad brought you to the church and water was splashed on you. And with that water and some words, God said, "I love you. You are my very precious child. I promise I will always be near, and I will hear you anytime you want to talk with me."

The other gift, the other sacrament, that we have from God is Holy Communion, or the Lord's Supper. In the last week that Jesus lived he had dinner with his closest friends. And when they were almost done, Jesus took some bread and passed it around to his friends, and said, "This is my body. For you." Then he passed the wine and said, "This is my blood. For you."

When you come to Communion and eat that little piece of bread and take that one sip of wine, you are not eating flesh or drinking blood. The bread is always bread and the wine is always wine. You are eating and drinking bread and wine. And yet Jesus says, "This is my body given for you and this is my blood shed for you."

And now we all say together, "How can this be?" I do not know. It is always bread and always wine, ordinary bread and ordinary wine. It does not change into something else. And yet Jesus says, "This is my body and this is my blood." How is that possible? I do not know. All I know is that I believe him. I believe Jesus. Jesus does come to us in the bread and wine because he says so. And I believe him.

The water in Baptism is not magic water. It is ordinary water. The bread and wine are not changed into flesh and blood. It is still ordinary bread and wine. But Jesus promises that you belong to him with that water. And Jesus promises to come to you in the bread and wine. And he does. Simply because he says so. And simply because we believe him.

Jesus says, "This is my body given for you and this is my blood shed for you."

Listen carefully when those words are spoken because those are very important words. For you. For you. For you.

Jesus is saying, "I was born in Bethlehem for you. I went about doing good, to show you what it is like to be a child of God, for you. When I died on that terrible cross, it was for you. When I was raised up from death to life, it was for you."

Those are the two most important words in Communion. For you. Hang on to those words. Know that Jesus is for you. Know that the Church is for you.

Even when we are not able to be together, and when we are not able to receive the bread and wine of Holy Communion, you still hear the words and you still know that Jesus is as near to you as the very breath you breathe.

When you like someone and you want to show that person you like him or her, you can go out and buy a present. But your love for that person is not dependent upon the gift, and that person knowing of your love is not dependent upon that gift. What counts is your love, and what counts for that person is he or she believing your love.

What counts is God's love and what counts is your believing that you are loved by the one who took some bread, broke it, gave it to his friends and said, "This is my body, given for you." Then took some wine and said, "This is my blood, shed for you." For you. For you. For you.

You've Got to Be Carefully Taught

In 1949 Richard Rodgers and Oscar Hammerstein produced a musical for Broadway entitled *South Pacific,* based on the book *Tales of the South Pacific* by James Michener. It was a big hit and a successful movie followed in 1958.

But *South Pacific* almost didn't make it to Broadway because of one song sung by the character Lieutenant Cable. It is preceded by a line saying racism is, "not born in you! It happens after you're born …."

You've got to be taught to hate and fear. You've got to be taught from year to year. It's got to be drummed in your dear little ear. You've got to be carefully taught.

You've got to be taught to be afraid of people whose eyes are oddly made and people whose skin is a diff'rent shade. You've got to be carefully taught.

You've got to be taught before it's too late before you are six or seven or eight to hate all the people your relatives hate. You've got to be carefully taught.

"You've Got to Be Carefully Taught" was subject to widespread criticism, judged by some to be too controversial or inappropriate for the stage. One legislator said the song justified interracial marriage and was a threat to the American way of life. In other words, this gentleman proved the truth of the song. Rodgers and Hammerstein said the song stays.

Prejudice: "A preconceived opinion that is not based on reason or actual experience."

Prejudice: A condition that is found in all of us.

I have forgotten large chunks of my life. But there are moments that are still vivid, events of long ago that do not seem so long ago, events even from my childhood. I remember the fire that burned down our barn in North Dakota when I was ten. I remember hitting our mailbox just after getting my driver's license. I remember where I was when I first heard the Everly Brothers sing, "Bye Bye Love."

And I remember sitting in the back sit of a car with my aunt and uncle and hearing my aunt, my very conservative, Norwegian, Christian aunt turn to me and speak of another human being as a "n word." Still makes me sad.

We confess Jesus as our Savior. He is also our Rabbi, our teacher. He came into this world because something is wrong with us. He came to open our eyes to see that truth, to teach us, and to give us the courage to fix it. It is what teachers do. If, as the song says, we can be taught to hate and to fear, then it must be true that we can be taught to be brave and to love.

Faith and love are not simply matters of the heart, but also of the mind and will. We look inside ourselves, see who we are, see the truth of us. And then we strive to do better, to be intentional about our speaking and our doing.

We can be taught to be kind, to speak with respect, to treat others in the way we wish to be treated. We can be taught to see others as having feelings, as being afraid, as wanting to be loved.

And we can teach our children to do the same.

It begins with the truth that we are all created in the image of God, that we are all God's children. No one is less.

Afraid and Lonely and Tired and Ticked

Jesus is pretty sure he is going to be killed. There are people, powerful people, religious people, who want him dead. He is scared and he wants to spend some time in prayer, so he takes three friends and goes to a place called Gethsemane. They have been together for a while now. These friends love Jesus and he loves them. Peter even says at one point, "Even though everyone else fails you, I won't. I would die for you." James and John nod their heads in agreement.

He wants time alone to pray, yet he wants his friends near. He asks them to stay close and stay awake. That is all he asks. But they fall asleep. Three times Jesus finds his friends sleeping. Finally, he says, "Enough!" In that one word, Jesus is saying, "I am tired and I am ticked. Enough!"

Contrary to what is sometimes depicted in paintings, Jesus did not go around with a halo over his head. He was a baby nursing at his mother's breast, a boy of 12 disobeying his parents, a young man standing before his elders in the synagogue, a man weeping at the news of a friend's death. He was a Jew, the son of a working man. He was a Rabbi, a teacher who loved helping others, and, according to some, a heretic. He was executed at the age of 33. He bled and he died.

Tired and ticked. I can relate. I have been there. Perhaps you have too. I get scared. Jesus got scared. I get hungry. He got hungry. I get tired. He got tired. I get angry. He got angry. One human being talking to another human being.

Years ago, one of our previous governors said, "I don't understand transgender people, have never visited with a transgender person." In response, a South Dakota high school senior stood in front of a television camera and asked this rhetorical question, "How does one talk to a transgender person?" Then answered, "I am a human being, the governor is a human being, so it is one human being talking to another human being."

I am not African American. I do not know what it is like to be a black man in America. I don't know what it is like to be Native American. I don't know what it is like to be a gay man in our society. I don't know what it is like to be poor. I don't know what it is like to be .... The list goes on. And that is the truth. I do not fully comprehend what it is like to be poor or gay or black or female.

And yet I am a human being. As is the gay man. As is the transgender student. As is the Native American. As is the woman who does not make enough to put food on the table for her children. One human being seeing another human being as a person, not a category. One human being talking to another human being. One human being helping another human being.

I often come back to these words written by William Shakespeare and spoken by Shylock in the Merchant of Venice: "I am a Jew. Hath not a Jew eyes? Hath not a Jew hands, organs, dimensions, senses, affections, passions? Fed with the same food, hurt with the same weapons, subject to the same diseases, healed by the same means, warmed and cooled by the same winter and summer, as a Christian is? If you prick us, do we not bleed? If you tickle us, do we not laugh? If you poison us, do we not die?"

Those words, out of the mouth of a Jewish man, could be spoken by a Christian or a Muslim or a Buddhist or an agnostic or an atheist. By a man or a woman. By an African American or a Norwegian.

Our humanity connects us to one another. And Jesus' humanity connects us to God. Jesus is how God comes to us. So God understands when we get tired or angry, when we are scared, when we suffer and when we die. God has been there. Because "the word became flesh and lived among us."

"What a friend we have in Jesus, all our sins and griefs to bear! What a privilege to carry everything to God in prayer! Can we find a friend so faithful ... Jesus knows our every weakness — take it to the Lord in prayer."

One human being talking to another human being.

Forgive Us Our Sins As We Forgive

There used to be a comic strip called "Calvin and Hobbes." Calvin is a six-year-old boy who carries around a stuffed tiger named Hobbes. When no one else is around, Hobbes is a real tiger who converses with Calvin. The strip reveals the power of a child's imagination. There is a bigger kid named Moe, who keeps beating up on Calvin at school. In the first panel of one strip, we see Calvin at his locker when Moe walks by and says, "You're dead at recess, Twinky."

Panel two, Calvin folds his arms, gets a serious, concerned look on his face and says, "I feel sorry for you, Moe. You must have some serious personal problems if this is how you relate to people."

Panel three, Moe swings his arm, there is a big POW, and we see Calvin's shoes flying and stars above his head.

Last panel, Calvin, now bruised and dirty, flat on his back, shoes off, says to us, "Then again, maybe he is just a world-class poop head."

Ain't it the truth? There are some people you cannot explain, you cannot excuse, and finally you decide they are just world-class poop heads. And we are supposed to forgive them.

There is a story in the gospel of Matthew (18:21-35) which begins with Peter coming to Jesus and asking, "Lord, if another member of the church sins against me, how often should I forgive? As many as seven times?" Jesus says, "Not seven times but I tell you 77 times."

My understanding is that in Jesus' day, the Jewish law said that one must forgive another three times. Peter doubled that and added another just for good measure. Seven times. That's generous. But Jesus disagrees. Not seven times, but 77 times. An older translation reads 70 times seven, or 490 times. But maybe it's not about math after all. Maybe it's about remembering.

After Jesus instructs Peter, he tells a story about a king who owns slaves. One slave owes the king a lot of money. The slave begs for mercy. The king takes pity and forgives the debt. The slave then goes out and finds a fellow slave who owes him some money. This guy also begs for mercy, but no mercy is shown. The king hears about this, brings the guy back and says, "Remember how I showed you mercy and yet you could not do the same for another."

The slave forgot. He had been forgiven an enormous debt. One talent was worth more than 15 years' wages, and he owed the king 10,000 talents. A fellow slave owed him 100 denarii. One denarius was one day's wage. The difference between the two debts is ridiculous, but the point is made.

Forgiveness is about remembering that you have been forgiven. By a friend. By a spouse. By your boss. By some stranger. Sometime in your life, you have been forgiven. You know what that feels like. You know what it did for you, how it freed you, took away that nagging feeling of guilt. The prison doors flung open.

There is a God who created you, who sustains you, who came to this world in the person of Jesus. You are accountable to this God for how you conduct your life and how you treat people. And if you have asked God to forgive you, and have heard the words of absolution, and trusted that God has indeed forgiven you, well, then forgiveness is about remembering.

When we pray the Lord's Prayer, one of the petitions is, "Forgive us our trespasses as we forgive those who trespass against us," or, "Forgive us our debts as we forgive our debtors."

St. Augustine called this the "terrible petition." For this is what we are praying: "I ask you, Father, deal with me as I deal with my brother or sister," or "I despise her, Lord, and the first opportunity I get to pay her back will give me great satisfaction. Deal with me, Lord, as I deal with her."

John Wesley — who with his brother, Charles, founded the

Methodist Church — had an encounter with a general, a man known for his pride. Wesley asked the general if he could forgive a man who was given a severe penalty for a minor infraction. The general said, "I never forgive!" Wesley replied, "Then I hope, sir, you never sin."

It is one thing to forgive someone who forgot to call you back or showed up a few minutes late, but what about that person who has really hurt you, betrayed your trust, said something that embarrassed you in front of others, or did something unspeakable?

When I was a working pastor in Vermillion, a university student came to see me. He said that there was someone who had done something to him, and he knew he needed to forgive; it was a part of his faith. But he said he couldn't do it. We talked and finally I said, rightly or wrongly, "Maybe for now, let Jesus forgive him. Let God forgive him. Let your faith allow that to happen. And then maybe there will come a time when you can also forgive, but for now let God do it."

Forgiveness is hard. It always costs. Frederick Buechner said that whether you are a person asking for forgiveness or the one who is asked to forgive, both parties must swallow the same thing: their pride. The pride which keeps us from forgiving is the same pride which keeps us from accepting forgiveness. But, he said, for both parties, forgiveness means the freedom again to be at peace inside one's own skin.

Jesus said, "When you are offering your gift at the altar, if you remember that your brother or sister has something against you, leave your gift there before the altar and go; first be reconciled to your brother or sister, and then come and offer your gift." (Matthew 5:23) I believe Jesus is saying that heaven and earth are connected.

And this, from Danish theologian Søren Kierkegaard (1813-1855): "Forgiveness does not change the past but it does enlarge the future."

Turning the World Upside Down

If you watch *Jeopardy,* you know there are three contestants, and at the end of the show the person winning the most money gets to come back the next day and play again for more money. The other two are done. I find myself thinking, "Why not let the winner go home and invite the person with the least amount of money to come back and try again?" In other words, turn the game upside down.

But that's not the American way. Losers go home and winners get to win some more. The workers get laid off or lose their pensions. The executives give themselves a bonus.

These words are found in the gospel of Luke, chapter 6, spoken by Jesus to the Church: "But I say to you ... love your enemies, do good to those who hate you, bless those who curse you, pray for those who abuse you. Give to everyone who begs from you .... Do to others as you would have them do to you."

A world turned upside down.

It is a part of the Christian faith that we either dismiss or forget. We are good at singing, "Jesus loves me, this I know ...." We confess boldly that Jesus died for our sins, was raised up from death to life, that he lives and has promised us forgiveness and eternal life in heaven.

But Jesus also instructs us in our daily walk. The Kingdom of God is not only about the promise of a life in heaven. It is about a life lived now. Jesus sets before us a world turned upside down and then gives instruction on how that might work.

I grew up in a family where certain things were just expected. There were things you did and did not do. We brushed our teeth, were polite to older people and those in authority. We went to church. We obeyed our parents. We didn't vote on that. It was expected. We had a benevolent dictator, and we called her Mom.

Jesus has expectations as well. "Love your enemies. Do good. Bless others. Pray for others, even those you might not care for so much. Give if you have something to give."

He is not asking us to vote on it. It is not one option among many. We are under orders.

Father William Bausch tells this story: There was a big drifter named George; wild hair, tattered pants, oversized food-stained T shirt. One Sunday morning George goes into a large, beautiful church. He finds no place to sit and no one makes room for him, so he sits on the floor in front of the pulpit. It gets quiet. Then the congregation's elderly head usher slowly makes his way down the aisle to George. He is elegant, always well dressed, and he walks with a cane, but he walks with confidence and authority. Everyone in the room knows that he will deal with George. It takes a while, but the old man finally gets to George. Then he lays down his cane, and with great difficulty lowers himself to sit on the floor with George, so that George does not sit alone.

I think that is what Jesus is talking about. He quietly and gently went about touching people's lives, and he told his followers to do the same, to sit with those who find there is no room for them in this world.

It's Christmas morning in London during World War II. Some American soldiers are walking and pass a building with a sign, "Queen Anne's Orphanage." A woman comes to the door and explains that most of the children there are orphans because their parents have been killed in the bombings.

There are no presents, no tree, but the soldiers go around wishing the children Merry Christmas and giving them what they have: a stick of gum, piece of candy, a nickel. Then one soldier notices a boy in the corner and asks, "Hey, what do you want for Christmas?" The child replies, "Will you hold me?"

When we gather in worship, it is in part to experience once again the healing that comes from Christ as we make confession of our wrongdoing, and our lack of doing, and receive forgiveness. And it is in part to encourage one another to not lose faith, to trust that we can be the disciples Jesus has called us to be, bringing healing and hope to those we meet in this world.

The church is, as it has always been, a communion of ordinary people, like you and me, living faithfully as best we can. If you are like me, there is a great sense of helplessness. We usually don't know what to do.

But the truth is, hurting people usually don't want advice or explanation, but simply want to be held and to be heard. We can do that. And when we do, we are turning the world upside down the way Jesus describes.

The stories of his raising the dead or walking on water or changing water into wine only confuse me because they seem so far away from what I have experienced in life. But those little scenes, those brief encounters with ordinary people who were considered of little value or importance still encourage and invite me.

For many, the Christian Church is irrelevant. It has nothing important to say and when it does say something good, often the actions of the church do not match the nice words. But people are still attracted to Jesus. They like what he says, and they like how he treats people. He always leaned towards inclusiveness. He always opened his arms to those the religious folk wanted to exclude. He noticed people and he paid attention to people. He was doing something that all of us can do.

Ordinary, common, everyday compassion. Turning the world upside down.

Because God Loves This World

In the movie *The Last Emperor*, the young child anointed as the last emperor of China lives a magical life of luxury with a thousand servants at his command.

"What happens when you do wrong?" the emperor's brother asks. "When I do wrong, someone else is punished," the boy king replies. To demonstrate he breaks a jar and one of the servants is beaten.

The gospels, the stories of Jesus, tell of a God who reversed that pattern. "For God so loved the world that he gave his only Son." Our faith is that Jesus died on that cross outside of Jerusalem for our sins; that in that cross, in that death, there is forgiveness. When the servants erred, the king was punished. Grace means that the giver has borne the cost. Because God loves this world.

Because God loves this world, your future is secure. Henry David Thoreau was dying from tuberculosis. It was 1862 and he was only 44. His aunt inquired if he was at peace with God. Thoreau replied, "I was not aware we had quarreled."

Because God loves this world, your status is established. An Irish priest saw an old peasant kneeling by the side of the road, praying. The priest said, "You must be very close to God." The peasant looked up, thought for moment, smiled and responded, "Yes, God is very fond of me."

Because God loves this world, God's glory is revealed in the ordinary. A son, one of 13 children, felt called to the priesthood. He became a monk. At the monastery at 2 a.m., all the monks gathered to sing. He felt close to God now that he was apart from the noise and busyness of the world. He wrote his father: "How wonderful it feels to be praising God when the world around me is asleep and I and my fellow seminarians are giving glory to God."

His father wrote back that he was glad that his son appreciated his life as a monk. But he remembered when the son was an infant, one of 13 children, and so as parents they too were often up at 2 a.m., giving glory to God in the care of their son and his brothers and sisters, even though they were not quite singing the Psalms.

It is often in the everydayness of life that we uncover God and God's graciousness, that we again and again discover that God loves this world.

God is there in the children fed, in the dishes done, in the comfort given, in the business conducted with integrity, in the seed planted and the harvest gathered, in the job well done, in the handshake and the welcome, in the patience of the parent helping with homework, in the neighbor helping neighbor, in the poor being welcomed, in the hug and the letter, in the ordinary moments that the world might miss, but God notices.

One of the reasons for gathering for worship is to get our vision adjusted, to see again, to celebrate the God we have bumped into all week and maybe not noticed. We worship God who came to us in Jesus, who reveals to us his graciousness in water and bread and wine, for such common stuff harbors the very presence of God.

It is easy to become cynical. So it is good to worship in a community of faith on a regular basis, to be encouraged once again to praise beauty and truth, to be invited once again to be open to grace at every turn of life, and to resolve again to practice forgiveness on a regular basis, because God loves this world.

Someone once said that God sent Jesus to play with his children. And though we did our best to get Jesus out of our lives, God raised him up from death, setting him free, giving life to him and, thereby, to you and to me, because God loves this world.

So live, dear reader. Live. And love this world too.

Leaving Church Early

Jesus says, "So when you are offering your gift at the altar, if you remember that your brother or sister has something against you, leave your gift there before the altar and go; first be reconciled to your brother or sister, and then come and offer your gift." (Matthew 5:23-24)

Well, this could mean quite a few of us leaving church early.

If you remember that there is something wrong between you and another. If you remember misspoken words, angry words. If you remember that something is broken with your brother, your sister, your friend. If you remember, then ….

Well, then leave your worship. Getting reconciled with family and friends is more important than coming to Church and praying.

Or maybe there is a connection between the two.

Vivian and I went to a local store recently. A sign at the entrance stated that masks were mandated. When we went to check out there was one person ahead of us. As he was leaving, we could see he was talking to the cashier, but we could not hear what he was saying. He left and we moved ahead. As we both seemed to notice some sadness in the woman's eyes, I asked if she was okay. She said the man was angry with her because he had to wear a mask. "Does this happen often?" "Yes," she said, "all the time."

This is who we are. This is what we do. Too often. That young woman did not make the rules, did not decide that the gentleman needed to wear a mask. But did he go to the store manager? No, this brave man took out his anger on a person who stands all day helping people with their purchases while making $10 per hour.

I have no way to prove this, but am pretty sure if I would have asked this gentleman, "Tell me, please, are you a Christian or are you Muslim or do you practice the Jewish faith, or perhaps you are an atheist?" Chances are, this being South Dakota, he would have replied, "I am a Christian, have been all my life."

We go to church on Sunday, we sing the hymns, listen to the scripture, ask God to forgive us, pray for the sick, and then on Monday we go yell at someone because we are having a bad day, or we are inconvenienced by having to wear a mask.

Shame on that man at the check-out counter. Shame on all of us when we treat other people as less. God's grace is no excuse for our bad behavior.

What we do counts for something. We can sing the hymns, pray the prayers, say amen to the sermon on Sunday, but if we go out on Monday and treat people like dirt, then it is for naught. Empty worship. Empty faith.

I do not live on an island all by myself. I live in community. What I do in community affects the people who live in this community with me. Therefore, Jesus' words, "if you remember" that there is something broken between you and another, then you need to take care of that now. That relationship with another child of God is as important as your relationship with God. Or perhaps one could say they are connected and cannot be separated.

Vivian and I were in the Hy-Vee parking lot. We returned to our car, put our groceries inside, started to get in when a woman came to the car facing us. She was parked so that if she opened her door we could not drive ahead. She said to Vivian, "Will you be okay if I open my door? If not, I can leave my door shut and step back, so you can drive forward." Vivian told her we were just fine and would back out. I stepped out of our car, and said, "That was so kind of you to think of us. Thank you." She said, "Well, I try to be kind." I liked her already. She reminded me of Jesus.

I invite you to hang on to the words of Henry James (1843-1916). "Three things in human life are important. The first is to be kind. The second is to be kind. And the third is to be kind."

Together Is a Beautiful Place to Be

On Thursday, August 4, there will be a seven-passenger rental van in Norfolk, Nebraska waiting for our daughter, Christin, who will drive the van to our home and then the three of us will continue our journey to the Minneapolis airport. There we will be joined by our son, Josh, and his two boys, Benjamin and Finn, who will have flown in from College Park, Maryland.

The six of us will continue our journey to northern Minnesota. There will be a cabin waiting for us at a town called Orr, population 211, located within the Kabetogama State Forest. We will stay for three nights. Then we will travel two hours south to Two Harbors, on the shore of Lake Superior with Gooseberry Falls State Park 13 miles to the northeast. We will stay at a house in Two Harbors for three nights before driving back to Minneapolis and South Dakota and Nebraska.

One day, while talking about the upcoming adventure, Josh said to his mother, "The main thing is that we will be together."

Perhaps that is a main thing about life. Together.

The English prefixes "syn" and "sym" are derived from the Greek and have the meaning of "with" or "together." So a synonym is a word that goes "together" with another word because it has a similar meaning. When clocks are synchronized, their times are placed "together" so that they all show the same time. You might feel sympathy for someone with a cold, suffering "together" with her. A Jewish house of worship is called a synagogue, which means a place where people are led "together" to worship.

And a symphony is a sounding "together" of instruments. A total of 44 instruments are played in a full orchestra. Each instrument can play alone and make beautiful music, but "together" something special happens.

There are Sunday mornings when I think it would be easy to stay home, skip church, maybe watch one of the Sunday morning services on television. I would hear the scriptures read and a sermon preached, hear some familiar hymns and maybe even a choir sing. Pretty much as if I had gotten in my car and driven to the building. But then I remember that I would miss the people. I would miss the smiles, the sound of children, the laughter, and the greetings. I would miss being together. That is what the local church is about. That is what much of life is about.

You have heard the words spoken to you and you have said them to others: "Remember, we are in this together." "It's kind of dark outside. Let's go out together." "I'll go with you to the doctor; we'll be together." "When you get to the party, look for me so we can sit together."

It is a word of kindness, of grace, of blessing. It's your mom holding your hand as you walk to the school bus for the first time. It's your bride looking into your eyes as you make promises before family and friends. It's family gathering at Christmas. It's a friend holding your hand as your stand over the grave of someone you have known your whole life.

For sure, we need food, clothing, shelter, but we also need friendship, laughter, quiet, rest, peace and hope. Jesus fed the hungry and gave sight to the blind. But he also took time to have conversation at the town well, to sit with friends and bless the children.

A child awakens in the middle of the night, crying out to her mother. The mother comes into the child's room and the child says, "I'm scared." The mother says, "There is nothing to be afraid of. There is no one in the closet, no one under your bed." The child says, "I know, but I am still scared." Now the mother knows no argument or evidence will work, so she simply says, "I am here with you." Together may not be an answer to the child's fear, but it is a loving response to the child.

When I would meet with family at the funeral home, I would never say, "It will be okay." I had no right to say such. But I could and did say, "I am here. I am with you."

I share with you words I wrote after visiting a friend in a care center several years ago. It is entitled "Her Wish."

Her days are spent in a wheelchair,
living in a place she would rather not be.
Her husband died last February.
Married for over 60 years.
I wish I could have died when
he died, she says,
and means it.
I picked him out, she says.
We were skating.
It was ladies' choice,
and I picked him out.
We have been together
ever since.
I wish I could have died
when he died.

Jesus says, "In my Father's house there are many dwelling places. ... I go to prepare a place for you ... so that where I am, there you may be also." (John 14:2-3)

"Together" is a gift shared one to another. The friend who calls from time to time, the parent who walked you to the bus so long ago, the daughter who takes your hand when getting up from a chair is not so easy anymore. The husband and wife who kept the promise for 60 years. "Together" is a gift.

And "together" is also a promise. The promise of a place prepared for us. The promise that once again we will be together.

Two Miracles

Soon afterwards Jesus went to a town called Nain, and his disciples and a large crowd went with him. As he approached the gate of the town, a man who had died was being carried out. He was his mother's only son, and she was a widow; and with her was a large crowd from the town. When the Lord saw her, he had compassion for her and said to her, "Do not weep." Then he came forward and touched the bier, and the bearers stood still. And he said, "Young man, I say to you, rise!" The dead man sat up and began to speak, and Jesus gave him to his mother. Fear seized all of them; and they glorified God, saying, "A great prophet has risen among us!" and "God has looked favorably on his people!" This word about him spread throughout Judea and all the surrounding country.

Luke 7:11-17

Two miracles that day.

"'Young man, I say to you, rise!' The dead man sat up and began to speak ...."

But before that, there is this: "When the Lord saw her ...."

We are told that "a large crowd went with Jesus," and there was also a large crowd with the funeral procession. Yet in the midst of two large crowds, Jesus sees her. Her. He saw her. One widow. One human being. One child of God.

He was doing it all the time. He noticed Matthew sitting at the tax table. He saw Zacchaeus up in the tree. He noticed Peter and James and John who were fishing. He saw the children with their mothers. Not any of these were high on the social or economic ladder. Children, tax collectors, fishermen. And widows. Jesus saw them.

Oh, to be seen. To have someone finally see you.

I was at Luther Seminary from 1965 to 1969. There were 100 men in our class. There were also three women.

They came with no promise of ordination, no promise that the Church would see them. Barbara Andrews. Dawn Proux. Beverly Burkum Allert.

Their presence at Luther Seminary and their intention to seek ordination prompted ALC President Fredrik Schiotz to ask the Lutheran Council in the USA to make a study of women's ordination. Dr. Schiotz saw them. Someone finally saw them. They had to wave first.

Three brave women who made this world better for other women, that is true. They also made better the whole Church of Jesus Christ.

A miracle is defined as a remarkable, extraordinary event, causing one to wonder, to be surprised, to smile. On that day long ago, there was a widow, a mother whose son was returned to her. Because Jesus saw her. I am pretty sure she was surprised. And pretty sure she smiled, laughed even.

Another meaning of miracle is "a wonderful example." So Jesus has set for us a "wonderful example." There are people who are considered unimportant, simply numbers to be counted, of little value. The work of the Church of Jesus Christ is to see them.

And not get distracted by the crowds.

So God created humankind in his image,
in the image of God he created them;
male and female he created them.
Genesis 1:27

SHE
she is eve
unique
her own self
equal to adam
she is ruth
widowed young
free to leave
choosing to stay
she is deborah
leader of a nation
she is hannah
persistent in prayer
she is mary
honoring God with her worship
she is martha
honoring God with her service
she is
sarah
rahab
rachel
elizabeth
mary of nazareth
mary magdalene
she is a samaritan woman
who meets a
jewish man
by the village well

and is treated as equal
she is mother teresa
opening our eyes
to see jesus
in the poor
she is rosa parks
with the courage
not to go to the back of the bus
she is malala
wise beyond her years
she is harriet tubman
who never lost a passenger
traveling on the road to freedom
she is toni morrison
who with words
holds up a mirror
to our racism
she is
helen keller
sally ride
jane goodall
ruth bader ginsburg
michelle obama
greta thunberg
she earns 79 cents
for every dollar
earned by him
she has more than
a 75 percent chance
of experiencing
sexual harassment
or verbal abuse
in her lifetime

she did not get
the right to vote
until 1920
yet
she will teach us
to listen
to disagree without anger
to weep without shame
she is tough
but not mean
she would rather
talk than fight
she is
your grandmother
your mother
your sister
your wife
your pastor
your friend
she is eve
unique
her own self
equal to adam

The Blessing

Carl always welcomed me as one would welcome an old friend. He was glad to see me. Carl was in a nursing home, in a unit for people with Alzheimer's disease. I never knew Carl before this terrible thief robbed him of his precious memories, and robbed his family of a husband, father and grandfather.

Knowing that truth made me sad, but it could not diminish the joy of visiting Carl, for the thief could not steal Carl's kindness, nor his complete and unconditional acceptance of me as an old friend, even though I had just recently come to know him.

"It's good to see you, Carl." "It's good to see you too." I never needed to fear that I would be judged lacking in some area of performance as a pastor. I never came at an inappropriate time. I never felt the need to find something to talk about. I never worried that I was repeating myself. Sometimes we just sat, comfortable with each other, as old friends will do.

It was one of my last visits with Carl before he died. We were in the dining room, crowded with other members of this special community. Most were just sitting, but some were walking and some were talking (not always to a specific listener).

Carl had a headache that day. I could tell it was hurting him. He kept his head down. As usual, our conversation came in small pieces. I asked and he answered. At the mention of Florence, his good wife, he lifted his head, and I saw again how much he loved her. She came often and each time she left, he knew he should go home with her. The illness could not steal all the memories.

When I was ready to leave, I asked Carl if I could give him a blessing. "Yes." I placed my hand on his head. "The Lord bless you and keep you, Carl. The Lord make his face to shine upon you and be gracious to you. The Lord look upon you with favor and give you peace, Carl. In the name of the Father and of the Son and of the Holy Spirit. Amen."

There was a woman sitting a few feet away. When I ended my words, she reached her hand in my direction, palm open, quietly pleading to me. "Give me that, give me some of that." I went to her, placed my hand on her head, and repeated the old, old words of blessing. It was nothing grand on my part, simply the messenger delivering God's message. In the midst of the confusion of living, God blessed two of his children.

A blessing is only grace. It demands no payment, nor promise. It is a parent tucking a child into bed, a teacher telling a student, "Well done." It is Jesus calling Matthew the tax collector to come, follow. It is saying to another, you have value. God is saying, "You are precious, you are mine."

God bless you. Yes, you.

You Don't Have to Walk on Water

I am guessing you know the story. Jesus' disciples are in a boat. A storm comes up. They spend the night riding it out. In the morning they see Jesus walking toward them on the water. "It's a ghost," they cry. Jesus shouts back, "No. It's okay. Don't be scared. It's me." And good old Peter shouts back, "Well, if it's you, let me come walk on the water to you." Jesus says, "Okay. Have at it."

So Peter gets out of the boat and starts walking toward Jesus, until he realizes, "I can't walk on water," gets scared and starts to go under. He cries out, "Lord, save me." Jesus takes hold of his hand and asks, "Why did you doubt?"

Peter's prayer was simple and direct. Help! Perhaps the most honest prayer we pray.

We pray it when we are raising our children, when we lose our job, when we get sick, when we are lonely or sad, when we lose someone or are afraid we will lose someone, and sometimes when we watch the news and see how we live in a world where we attempt to solve our problems by killing one another or we see once again that nature can be cruel and uncaring.

As disciples of Jesus, we gather in our boats, our churches, not so brave, but taking a risk once in a while. When Peter said to Jesus, "Command me to come to you on the water," Jesus responded, "Come."

Maybe there are times when you should pray the same prayer. Maybe there are times when you should ask your Lord to command you to come, step out onto a stormy sea. Maybe there are times when you see something wrong in your world and someone needs to say something or do something, and maybe that someone is you. But you, like all those around, are afraid, so you need pray. "Lord, command me to come. Command me to step out of a place of safety and dare enter the stormy sea."

You know it will be scary, and you know you can't walk on water. But you don't have to. You just need to step out of the boat. Do the best you can. Call out to Jesus for help.

Sure, Peter failed in his attempt. But the other disciples didn't even try. Peter tried.

Jackie Robinson was the first African American to play for a major league baseball team, the Brooklyn Dodgers. He said it was a terrible first year; fans yelled racial slurs everywhere they played. But a miracle happened in Cincinnati. The fans, as usual, were shouting insults when there was a delay in the game. Pee Wee Reese walked across the diamond, put his arm around Jackie, and all the world saw. Robinson knew then that he would make it. That short walk and that embrace was a small miracle.

Pee Wee Reese, as Jackie Robinson had already done, stepped out of the boat, out of a place of safety onto the stormy sea, and made a difference.

When I was working as a pastor, I would get calls at 3:00 in the morning to come to the hospital. I didn't really feel like getting dressed and going out the door at 3:00 in the morning, but I did it anyway. Not because of my great compassion, but because I was under orders. My Lord bid me to come, to get out of the boat. Too often, we speak in the Church about feelings, about emotion, but it seems to me that Jesus is about doing more than feeling. There are people hurting everywhere, and we are under orders to do something about it, whether we feel like it or not.

Every one of you can get out of the boat, out of your safety zone and take a short walk in this stormy world. You don't have to succeed. But it would be good if you tried, like Peter, to do something brave and foolish, to do something good for someone.

A little boy was walking with his father on a slippery, snow packed road. Father said, "Let me take your hand." The boy said no and soon slipped and fell. As he got up the father said, "Let me take your hand." "No papa, I will take hold of your finger." Again, he slipped, and since he could not hold on to the finger of his father, again he fell. When he got up, the boy said to his father, "You better take my hand, Papa."

Let God take your hand. Let God love you. Just the way you are. No perfection. Just a child of God trying to make the world a little better for all of God's children.

There will come times when you feel unable to take God's hand, unable to believe, but know at those times that God has hold of you. Jesus reached out and caught Peter, not because of his great faith, but because he needed rescue.

In the same way, Jesus fed people and healed people not because they were nice or deserved it or earned it. He fed them because they were hungry and healed them because they were sick.

Jesus ends up in the boat with the disciples, with the Church, and there they worship him, declaring him to be the Son of God. We worship him as they did, and we take our cue from him, doing his work in this world. We, too, will feed the hungry, care for the sick, comfort the lonely and reach out to the stranger because we are His body, the body of Christ in the world. Perhaps of little faith, perhaps afraid at times, perhaps foolish, but we know who will rescue us, lift us up, and stay with us always.

No, we need not walk on water. We need not get it right all the time. We need not know perfection. We need not pretend how brave we are. We need not have such great faith.

We need only to know who to have faith in. And then listen for his voice of command. "Come," he says. "Come." And he also says to us, as he said to those disciples in that boat long ago, "Take heart, it is I, do not be afraid."

The Incidents of the Grass Can and the Water Sprinkler

Twice. In one week.

The first time was the incident of the grass can. In all the years we lived in Watertown, I never missed a pickup of our garbage or cut grass. I put the cans out between 7 and 8 in the morning and take the empty cans back to the garage in the afternoon. Like clockwork.

But one afternoon when I went to put the cans away, I saw that grass was still in the green can. I checked my neighbor's green can. Empty. They missed me. How could they have missed me?

I could have let it go. There was room in the can for another week. But I decided to call, to point out the error of their ways. The gentleman on the other end of the line patiently listened to my complaint, then asked for my address. After a brief time, he came back with the news that the green cans on our street had been picked up at 6:40 that morning. I had forgotten about the new previously announced schedule. I managed a thank you as I quickly hung up. Yes, it was someone's fault, just not the someone I expected.

That was Wednesday. The following Sunday it rained. When the rain stopped, I decided to go for some ice cream. As I drove to my destination, I noticed at least three yards being watered by sprinklers. I thought to myself, "I don't understand why people don't turn off their sprinklers when it is raining. How dumb."

On Tuesday morning, I woke up to another beautiful rain. I looked out my window and saw that the sprinklers, my lawn sprinklers, were watering the backyard in unison with the rain. I forgot to turn them off the night before, even after hearing the forecast for rain. How dumb.

There is this word from James in the New Testament: "You must understand this, my beloved: let everyone be quick to listen, slow to speak, slow to anger." (James 1:19)

I was quick to speak, quick to judge. Twice in one week. And those are the times I remember.

For what purpose? To make myself feel better? "I might not have it all together, but I certainly am not as bad as so and so." I build my righteousness on the back of another child of God.

James continues, "If any think they are religious, and do not bridle their tongues but deceive their hearts, their religion is worthless." (James 1:26)

And more. "How great a forest is set ablaze by a small fire! And the tongue is a fire. With it we bless the Lord and Father, and with it we curse those who are made in the likeness of God. From the same mouth come blessing and cursing. My brothers and sisters, this ought not to be so." (James 3:5b-6a, 9-10)

Yes, James, this ought not to be so. But too often, it is. And with our technology and social media platforms, we can attack another child of God without taking responsibility for our words, without even looking into the person's eyes and seeing their tears.

One of the more discouraging discoveries for me is to read posts on social media written by people I know, people who bear the name of Christ, who now write horrible words about other people. I find myself asking, "Is this who you really are? Has it all been an act?"

We can scream at another child of God, call her names, threaten her, because "we would never do something like that." We can damn a whole community of people or judge a religious faith because someone in that community or someone of that faith did something terrible.

But most of the time, it is simpler. It is about the words we speak to our spouse or our children, a neighbor, or someone in our community. Harsh words come easily. Contrary to James' admonition, we are slow to listen, quick to speak, quick to anger.

God forgive us.

I was watching a Christian news show. The host was talking about some war in some faraway place, and then he turned to a reporter on the scene. The reporter said, "Terrible situation here, but, of course, we know that God is in control."

I remember yelling back, "People are killing one another, and God is in control? You have got to be kidding. God is in control?" We are not puppets on a string. We make choices. We don't simply make mistakes, we choose. We don't just stumble, we decide. We are accountable for our words, our lives.

There is an old Good Friday hymn, *Ah, Holy Jesus*, which includes the words, "Who was the guilty? Who brought this upon thee? Alas, my treason, Jesus, hath undone thee. 'Twas I, Lord Jesus, I it was denied thee; I crucified thee."

We choose.

I tend to lean Lutheran, so a quote from Martin Luther: "A Christian is free, subject to none. And a Christian is the most dutiful servant of all, subject to everyone."

Catching a Glimpse of Jesus

My friend went through a divorce. Like most who have traveled that road, he did not plan such when he got married and it came as a terrible surprise to him. He felt he had failed.

He said that for a long time after the divorce, he would go to church but was unable to hear the sermon or participate in the liturgy or sing the hymns. He said that his hope was gone. Nothing spoke to him of God's forgiveness or love. Except. There was an except. Except for the supper of our Lord. It was there, he said, in the simple act of receiving that plain food and hearing the remarkable words, "the body of Christ given for you, the blood of Christ shed for you," that he heard and perhaps tasted the goodness and the forgiveness of God. In that supper he found some peace and hope was restored. My friend caught a glimpse of Jesus in the breaking of the bread.

There is this beautiful story in the gospel of Luke (Luke 24:13-35) that takes place after the death of Jesus. Two of his disciples are walking along when Jesus joins them. Of course, they don't recognize him; they saw him dead and buried. They tell this stranger about Jesus, about his death, and then they say, "but we had hoped." Past tense. Jesus had given them hope, but now hope was dead and buried.

When they stop for the evening, the two disciples invite the stranger to join them for supper. During the meal he takes bread, gives thanks, breaks it and gives the bread to the two disciples. Then we are told that "their eyes were opened, and they recognized him." There was something in that action that stirred the memory. Then in the same sentence, "and he vanished out of their sight." Just a glimpse. A tiny bit of grace. But it is enough. Their hope is renewed. They had earlier invited him to stay, but he does not stay. But it's okay. They only needed a sign, something they could hang on to, something to keep them, to give them hope.

They go back to Jerusalem, to tell the other disciples. They become witnesses. They who had lost hope, who could only say, "but we had hoped," now have their hope renewed and they become witnesses.

Rabbi Abraham Heschel wrote, "There are no proofs for the existence of God, there are only witnesses."

In a story by Dostoevsky, "The House of the Dead," there are these words: "That is why every convict in Russia, whatever prison he may be in, grows restless in the spring with the first kindly rays of sunshine. Yet they dream at least of how they might escape and where they might escape to and comfort their hearts with the very desire, with the very imagination of it being possible. Imprisonment would be unbearable without hope. Without hope one cannot live."

Jürgen Moltmann: "Hope is nothing else than the expectation of those things which faith has believed to have been truly promised by God. ... Faith is the foundation upon which hope rests, hope nourishes and sustains faith." So it follows that when hope is gone, faith will soon vanish. "Without hope one cannot live."

When Harry Truman served in World War I, he said letters from home were a sign that he was not forgotten, that he was loved.

My friend needed such a sign, so he put himself in a place, at the table of our Lord, hoping to catch a glimpse of Jesus, and he did. It was enough to keep him. It was not magic. It was not pretend. It was not wishful thinking or the power of positive thinking. It was real. It was faith. It was hope restored.

Martin Luther said that Christ is both hidden and revealed. Even after Christ's entrance into our lives, we do not feel unfailingly secure. "Stay with us," the two implore. We would like some certainty. He did not stay. They would learn to live by faith, as we too live by faith, but faith needs hope, a glimpse of God once in a while. Even if it is only a simple, plain thing, like the breaking of bread.

Or a word, or a hug. She had lost her husband the week before. She came back to worship, and no one knew what to say, so no one said anything. Then a friend came to her, wrapped her arms around her, wept with her. It didn't change the truth of her husband's death, but it gave her a glimpse of Jesus, and it helped.

This Place

We were going to find this place.
We had read about this place.
We thought this would be a good place to visit.
We drove and found a sign.
The sign indicated there actually was such a place.
A place to drive to, a place to find.
But we could not find this place.
We missed our destination.
But we kept driving anyway
and we reached another place.
It was a very nice place.
We were glad we found this new place.
Sort of like life.

This Faith We Have

We could have it all wrong.
Simply a tale told by fools for fools.
Deceived.
No virgin birth.
No angel song.
No empty tomb.
A teacher long dead.
Yes, it could be so.
Nothing.
And we all will turn to dust.
We could have it all wrong.
But still.
But still.
It has been a good way to live.
And perhaps we have it all right.
It is faith you know.
And it could be true.
We could have it all right.

Let the Children Come and Come and Come

I have grown weary of death. Vivian and I have lived in different communities, served different congregations, so we have formed many friendships over the years. And now on an almost weekly basis I hear of another friend's passing.

I remember when my father and Vivian's mother reached the age I am now, lamenting the loss of friends. And I remember a conversation with a friend who is now in his ninth decade talking about losing all his hunting buddies.

Recently I was visiting with some of my seminary classmates via Zoom, planning an upcoming gathering. We were talking about a possible program, and I said I hope we don't spend our time together talking about loss and death. I am pretty sure they became concerned about me. But I have grown weary of death.

And then along came Pam. Pam Brockberg is the Education Director at Trinity Lutheran Church where Vivian and I worship. Pam asked if I would like to help with Vacation Bible School. It would be a Family VBS for three evenings, two hours per evening. I would lead an opening devotion or lesson and close with prayer and a blessing. Pam would take care of the rest. Why not? It would be my gift to the Church and maybe to the children.

I was wrong. It was the children who gifted me.

For those six hours there was no death. There was only life. During the lesson, they listened. During the prayers, they prayed with me. During the games, they laughed and ran and screamed. There was noise and there was kindness and there was faith. It was remarkable. And it was life.

There is a brief story in the gospel of Matthew. Jesus is teaching and some parents come with their children in the hope that he will bless them. The disciples begin to push the parents and kids away, but Jesus welcomes them.

I think I understand that story better now. Jesus needed those kids as much as they needed him. They were life. To bless them, to look into their eyes, to hear their voices was to touch and see and hear life. "This is what the kingdom of God looks like," he said.

I do realize that when a parent is amid the daily task of caring for a child, it is too often simply hard work. "When will this ever end?" "I need to get away for a while." "Help!"

But when one looks back, as Vivian and I do, it seems so flitting. All those difficult times are swallowed by the joy and laughter and memories that still hold us. It was life that we held in our arms and hearts and lives for those too few years.

Vivian and I were at a grocery store a few days ago. As we passed the meat counter, a woman was waiting to be helped. Her daughter, who looked about five years old, was waiting with her. She was singing and dancing by herself as she waited with her mother. While all the adults in that space were looking glum, this child was enjoying life. And in so doing, she was giving life.

I write these words to tell you about the gift I was given for six hours in August, but also to express my appreciation to those children who presented me with that gift.

I name them now in the hope that a parent or grandparent or friend will read these words and tell the child of my appreciation. I am pretty sure they did not even realize what they did for me, but maybe someday they will understand.

So thank you Norah, Dawson, Brayden, Kolden, Cale, Henry, Ava, Ellis, Kollins, Will, Jack, Emmett, Lily, and Jada.

Always remember you are Jesus' treasure and for six hours, because of you, I saw only life.

The Holy Man

The holy man is coming out of his house
on Monday morning, hooked to his dog,
walking over the grass, stopping
as the dog squats.
Yesterday the holy man stood in
a holy place, held in his hands
the bread and wine of the
Holy Sacrament. Today he is out
in the world cleaning up shit.
It is what holy men do.

Perhaps Not As Easy Or As Simple As It Used To Be

I believe I have become a grumpy old man.

There is this commercial that begins with the announcer saying, "We know that men have evolved." Every time, I yell at the television, "No, we have not!"

I have never known life without the Church, without a faith in God. It's as much a part of me as breathing. I was born into a family of Christians. We didn't talk about it much. But then we are Norwegians. We didn't do a lot of hugging either. It was just who we were. We attended church every Sunday morning. I attended Sunday School, went through Confirmation, knew my pastor like he was family.

I never considered another path, another way of living. And I have no regrets. I am thankful for those who came before, grandparents, parents, other older relatives, thankful for their faith, the way they conducted their lives. Thankful that their faith in God was passed on to me.

At the same time, this old man gets discouraged.

At worship we confess, "I believe in God, the Father Almighty, Creator of Heaven and earth." At that same worship service, we might join together and sing, "Jesus loves me, this I know, for the Bible tells me so."

Yet one evil person seems to be almightier than God. People all over the world pray. We pray that this killing, this destroying of a nation will be done. But it is not done. Even the children, the children that Jesus loves, are being separated from their parents, are suffering and dying.

Does not God care? Does not God see and hear? "My God, my God, why?"

One of my teachers at seminary said, "We thank God for the good. We do not blame God for the bad." There is truth there, but at this point it doesn't help me very much.

I am so weary of the terrible things we do to one another. And I want God, this almighty God, who loves this world, to do something about it.

Christopher de Vinck, in his book, *The Power of the Powerless*, tells this story:

> One spring morning my 5-year-old son, David, and I were planting bushes along the side of the garage. A neighbor joined us for a few moments. David pointed to the ground. "Look Daddy, what's that?" "A beetle," I said. David was impressed and pleased with the discovery of this fancy, colorful creature. Then my neighbor lifted his foot and stepped on the insect. "That ought to do," he laughed. David looked at me, waiting for an explanation, a reason.
>
> That night, just before I turned off the light in his bedroom, David whispered, "I liked that beetle, Daddy." "I did too," I whispered back.

De Vinck concludes by writing, "We have the power to choose."

Intellectually, I suppose, I do have some understanding of why this world is so full of hurt. We have the power to choose. A dictator chooses to invade another country. A husband chooses to be unfaithful to the woman he made a promise to. A guy chooses to steal gas from some stranger's car. In my head I can explain this broken world. It's on us.

But my heart still aches. So I write these words to lament, to weep. I do not understand why this almighty and full-of-love God does not answer our prayers, does not put an end to all the hurtful and hateful things we do to one another. If God is in control, why does life seem so random? And why does this God I have believed in since my beginning seem so silent?

There is certainly much good in this world. There are people all around taking care of this planet and one another. I know that truth as well. And that gives me hope.

But I also believe we have reason to grieve, reason to question. At times I am that child who liked that beetle, and who just before sleep wonders why someone thought it was okay to destroy life and even took pleasure in it.

He Asks Not

— For Jim Boline, pastor and friend. I wrote these words for his ordination service on July 2, 1989, at Trinity Lutheran Church, Vermilion, South Dakota.

He asks not for our success,
nor our power.
He looks not for great achievements,
nor victory.
He seeks not our fine ideas,
nor our wisdom.
He bids us follow him,
and then turns — face set — and goes to Jerusalem.

By Faith

"… for we walk by faith, not by sight." — II Corinthians 5:7

We walk by faith.
We do not walk knowing.
We walk believing.
We do not know,
for if we did,
it would not be faith.
We walk by faith.

It is a good way to walk.
It can be a cure for self-righteousness.
It can be a cause for conversation.
It can be a beginning of good things.

For most of the important stuff of life is by faith:
friendship,
love,
marriage,
forgiveness.

We walk by faith, not by sight.
We walk by faith.

Precious Lord, take my hand.

A Glory That Is Found in the Living of Each Day

It is called the "prosperity gospel." Preachers like Joel Osteen and his Lakewood Church in Houston, Texas. One of the catchphrases is "plant a seed, reap a harvest." In other words, give and you will be blessed. God wants to bless you, but you need to prove your faith by giving. You need to trust God, then God will trust you with financial blessing, because God wants you to be wealthy. God wants you to be successful.

Once upon a time, a young man in college wrote a presentation called, "10 Commandments for Rearing Children." He graduated, got married, a child was born, and he changed his talk to "10 Rules for Rearing Children." A few years later, after his child started school, he changed his talk again to "10 Suggestions for Rearing Children." The child entered junior high and once again the father changed his talk to, "10 Helpful Hints for Rearing Children." When his child entered high school, the man quit giving his talk. Because sometimes our dreams bump into real life.

There is this little exchange in the gospel of Mark, chapter 10. "James and John, the sons of Zebedee, come to Jesus and say, 'Teacher, we want you to do for us whatever we ask of you.' And Jesus says to them, 'What is it you want me to do for you?' And they say to him, 'Appoint us to sit, one at your right hand and one at your left, in your glory.' But Jesus says to them, 'You do not know what you are asking.'"

Papa Zebedee's two boys have a dream of glory. Someday there will be a king and a kingdom, and they want a share in it. Prosperity gospel.

There will come a day when James and John will see their king in his glory, but he will be hanging from a cross, his crown will be made of thorns, and the men on his right and on his left will be criminals.

James and John don't get it. Not yet, anyway. But they will discover that to follow Jesus is to follow one who takes off his cloak, wraps a towel around his waist and washes the feet of his friends. This is our king. This is what he is about, and so this is what his Church is about.

The glory of Jesus is a glory found in living, not separated from the world, but very much involved in the world. I surmise that Joel Osteen, seeing the world from his $10 million mansion, has no idea what it is like to live in the world of most of his congregation. I would argue that he does not understand Jesus any more than James and John understand Jesus.

"When you come into your glory, we want to be with you," the brothers say. Jesus replies, "You are with me now and this is my glory. Watch me. This is what my glory is all about."

Albert Schweitzer once said to a graduating class, "I don't know what your destiny will be, but one thing I know: the only ones among you who will be happy are those who have sought and found a way to serve."

"The Velveteen Rabbit" is a story about a boy who receives a toy rabbit at Christmas. The rabbit lives in a nursery and talks to the other toys. The mechanical toys feel superior and pretend they are real because they have springs and can move. One day Rabbit asks old Skin Horse, who is the oldest and wisest of the toys, "What is real? Does it mean having things that buzz inside you and a stick out handle?" "Real isn't how you are made," replies the horse, "it is the thing that happens to you when a child loves you for a long, long time. Then you become real." Rabbit asks, "Does it hurt?"

"Sometimes," says the horse, "but when you are real you don't mind being hurt."

Rabbit asks, "Does it happen all at once like being wound up bit by bit?" "It doesn't happen all at once like being wound up, you become. It takes a long, long time. That is why it doesn't happen often to those who break easily or have sharp edges or who have to be carefully kept. Generally by the time you are real most of your hair has been loved off, your eyes are out, and you get loose in the joints and very shabby. But these things don't matter at all, because once you are real, you can't be ugly, except to people who don't understand."

So the velveteen rabbit was loved by the boy, dragged around the garden, left in the dew, and became shabby. One day the nurse tried to throw the bunny away, but the boy said, "You can't do that. He isn't a toy. He's real."

James and John were looking for a glory in the future, something up ahead, some kingdom out there, but Jesus invites them into a glory that is found in our living of each day.

Alice Childress (1916-1994), playwright and novelist, said, "Life is just a short walk from the cradle to the grave, and it sure behooves us to be kind to one another along the way."

When someone messes up, does something really stupid, something wrong, we might say, "Well, he's only human, you know." But I wonder. Jesus was only human. So when you do something good, something that helps another, something that is beautiful or kind, maybe then we should say, "Well, he's only human, you know."

Our society preaches and teaches self-care. Be good to yourself, take care of yourself. Jesus teaches that God cares about you, and you are meant to care for one another. Jesus does not teach self-care. Jesus is all about other-care.

What you do with your life matters.

Jesus

I think I understood God better when I was a child. The longer I live, the less I understand. I am baffled by God's way in the Old Testament, destroying nations on behalf of one nation. Baffled by God's silence in a world full of troubles.

It's an old question, but I still ask. If God is all powerful and full of goodness, then why? God too often seems like an absent parent, not noticing that we are doing terrible things to one another, and to ourselves.

So I hear Jesus' prayer from the cross. "My God, my God why …?"

But then I read again the story of Jesus. Then I see again his followers at work in the world today, doing good. And I realize once again that I like Jesus. Good storyteller. Great with kids. Sits down to dinner with all the relatives. Treats women as equals. Pays attention to those considered less.

I get Jesus. Jesus gives me hope. Jesus keeps me.

Jesus. The church gathers in that name, has a mission, does ministry in that name. What binds us together, breaks down barriers, comforts us, is that name.

In my study there are memories all around, pictures and books and ancient relics from my childhood. There will come a day when I leave them behind and they will belong to another. So what do I take with me? I will have my name. When all else fades, when all else no longer matters, I will still have my name.

And when your time on this earth is done, you will have your name. When your family and friends gather to comfort one another, they will speak your name and weep. A good name. An honorable name. A memorable name.

But another name will also be spoken. Jesus. That name is joined to your name and that name dares to give us hope. What you have when your world slips away, when someone else gets all your toys, are two names. Your name and his name.

It is enough.

"We are beggars. This is true."
Martin Luther

While Out Walking

While out walking one cool morning,
I passed a rabbit sitting alone.
He happened to be eating breakfast.
"Good morning, Rabbit,"
I said with a smile.
"Good morning," said he,
with his mouth full of green.
"May you have a good day," said I.
"May you also," said he.
And while Rabbit
finished his breakfast,
I walked on,
feeling even better than before.
I hoped he felt as good as I
for our meeting.

About the Author

Why Old Men Weep in the Morning is Gary Westgard's third and final book. The author died November 12, 2022, just as he was preparing to publish this collection.

Gary was born in Rugby, North Dakota, in 1940. When he was 10 years old, his family moved to Longview, Washington. After high school, he attended the Lutheran Bible Institute in Seattle, Washington, and Waldorf College in Forest City, Iowa. He graduated from Pacific Lutheran University in Tacoma, Washington, with a degree in literature.

After graduating from Luther Seminary in St. Paul, Minnesota, Gary served as pastor in Laurel, Nebraska. He then became a South Dakotan, serving churches in Gayville, Meckling, Vermillion, and Watertown. He was always a writer, and found more time to share his literary talents as he grew older.

Gary and his wife Vivian moved to Yankton in 2018.

They have two children — Christin, who is married to Dean, and Joshua, who has two sons, Benjamin and Samuel Finn.

May he rest in peace.

Made in the USA
Monee, IL
11 December 2024